George Hirsch!

LIVING IT UP!

Also by George Hirsch

GRILLING WITH CHEF GEORGE HIRSCH

KNOW YOUR FIRE

ADVENTURES IN GRILLING

GATHER ROUND THE GRILL

RECIPES FOR A
HEALTHY ACTIVE LIFE

M. Evans and Company, Inc.
New York

M. Evans and Company, Inc.
216 East 49th Street
New York, New York 10017

ISBN 0-87131-924-1

Book Design by Rik Lain Schell

9 8 7 6 5 4 3 2 1

Printed in the United States of America

DISCLAIMER

The information in this book is not intended to take the place of any medical advice. It reflects the author's experiences, studies, research, and options regarding a healthy lifestyle. Before using the recipes and advice in this book, consult with your physician or health-care provider to be sure they are appropriate for you.

All materials included in this publication are believed to be accurate. The publisher and author assume no responsibility for any health, welfare, or subsequent damage that might result from the use of these materials.

For Dori, all my love—Osu!

CONTENTS

ACKNOWLEDGMENTS

The creative process of the *Living it Up!* book was years in the making. Thanks to my many loyal readers and television friends, I am blessed with having the opportunity of sharing my experiences in writing this book for you. Also, I offer my thanks to those whom I may have omitted in this acknowledgment—please excuse any oversight.

Ninety million plus households. Is that all? My gratitude and admiration to Denise DiPaolo. You are a source of great motivation and constant energy within this project. Your shared vision of a creative future and belief in the plan has brought great inspiration to this work. Denise, you are one of the most talented persons I have ever met, and yes, *GH Meats* is my favorite video!

I offer my appreciation to Lloyd Jassin who wears many hats as counsel, agent, director of business development for Hirsch Productions, a co-executive producer for *GEORGE HIRSCH Living It Up!*, and a friend who will laugh with me during stressful times. I am thankful you understand that a walk to the fitness room is not a complete workout!

Traveling so much requires me to surround myself with people who will make me feel at home. My publisher and the whole team at M. Evans and Company, including George DeKay and Rik Lain Schell, provided the attention to this work to make it a great success. Thanks for making me feel at home.

PJ Dempsey, my editor, will call me with a laundry list of questions that require immediate attention to make our deadline. Not only do we make the deadline with minutes to spare, but she brings a fresh approach to what could be a tough schedule. PJ, this is what *Living it Up!* is all about. Thanks for believing in this work and supporting all my thoughts and words through the writing process. Let's schedule a date in the future so I can answer all your questions.

Marlene Koch, R.D., is one of the most talented nutritionists I have ever encountered. It was a delight to be in your nutrition refresher course and have you join me in *Living it Up!* I said I enjoyed the class and would call!

Living It Up! will continue for many years due to its Internet home at Centerseat.com. Scott Harmolin, Lee Haddad, Mark Haefeli, Terry Baker, and David Levine are a great interactive team to work with. Visit the home of Centerseat and you'll see just how talented they all are!

For all at WLIW including Terrel, Tom, Nick, Susan, Roy, Luanne, and especially Laura Savini. Laura, you are always there; I owe you more than two lunches. Honestly, Laura I didn't put the (L) in the listing.

For Chris, who always has us covered, no problem! Norm, all in our crew and those who watch my shows know that you are one of my kindest friends. Any who have had an opportunity to meet you can attest to why. Carol has believed in me and this project from the beginning and deserves my warmest appreciation for always being there. Steve and all the rest of my television production crew know how to define *Living it Up!* while taping or not. Always take the time to scout the sun and the lake.

Randy and Belinda are key in working with me to make the *Living It Up!* words become visually entertaining for millions on television. The positive impact this will provide will be beyond any possible measure. Let's do it again, and again, and again. . . .

I can live it up not only because I am physically stronger and mentally focused, but because I have met my biggest obstacle in testing my heart as well. My appreciation to my friends and training partners at TSK for always supporting me on and off the mat. OSU Sensei Doonan for taking me to the next level, with thanks from Sempai!

Living It Up! is the result of unending support and love from many, but none as much as my family. This creative work was achieved because of your beliefs in me. With all my love and thanks to Diane, Celine, Tom, Bob, Val, Trisha, Kevin, Angela, Brian, Michael, Nancy, and Tim. Moe, I am very lucky to be back home with you.

JoAnn, thanks for taking great care of the Dor. . . .

Not a day goes by that my thoughts of my mother Polly and father George are not with me. You may be gone but are never forgotten. Your love and upbringing have enabled me to share with millions of readers and viewers over the years and offer them all an opportunity to *Live it Up!*

"If I can do it, I know you can do it!"
George Hirsch

ACKNOWLEDGMENTS

HOW TO USE THE RECIPES AND MENU PLANS

I have developed these recipes to help you in your quest for a healthy active life. Included in the recipes are lots of fresh and flavorful ingredients which, along with healthy cooking techniques such as grilling, provide for naturally healthful meals. The recipes have been lowered in fat, but are full of fiber and other essential nutrients.

These recipes were created so that you may adapt them to add variety to your diet or to suit your personal taste. By adapting a recipe I mean that common-sense substitutions can be made—using foods such as skinless chicken for turkey or one type of fish or vegetable for another you prefer. You will also find a chapter in this book titled Stocking the Pantry. This chapter contains a list of nonperishable foods, herbs, spices, and flavorings that you should always have on hand when preparing meals ar home. I suggest that you preview the recipes a few days in advance to ensure that you have all the ingredients you will need for a particular dish.

As you begin to prepare and cook the recipes, take the time to notice how the ingredients work in combination with one another and the variety of textures, flavors, and tastes I have included in each dish. Being aware of these elements will help you to begin experimenting on your own with new recipes or creating variations of my recipes. For your convenience, most of the recipes have been incorporated into the 30-Day Menu Plan.

The 30-Day Menu Plan is designed to keep your body fueled throughout the day so you can keep moving in your new active life. It has also been designed with your health in mind; like the recipes, it is low in fat but high in fiber and nutrients. (And, of course, in flavor!) The Menu Plan is meant to be flexible. Once you have completed the 30-Day Menu Plan, you can begin on your own to substitute one recipe for another or to make substitutions for an entire day, if you wish. You will still be on the right track to a healthy, active life.

Nutritional Analysis

Nnutritional analysis is included with each recipe to help guide you through a healthy daily eating plan. (Recipes were analyzed using the smallest specified portions. Optional ingredients were not included.) The following key to the abbreviations used in the Nutritional Analysis is calculated on a per-serving basis too help you ensure that your substitutions for other items on the menu plan are truly equivalent choices.

You may also utilize this information to ensure your personal daily needs are being met. Since your personal needs are based on many factors, including your weight, age, gender, and activity level, it is best to consult a nutritionist or other medical care provider trained in nutrition to determine your exact needs. Before starting the 30-Day Menu Plan, you should also consult with your specialist if you have a current medical condition.

The 30-Day Menu Plan averages 2,000 to 2,200 calories a day. It contains 90 to 100 grams of protein, 20 to 30 grams of fiber, and 2,500 milligrams of sodium. The fat represents only 20 to 25 percent of calories. Daily caloric intake can be increased simply by eating larger portions of the specified items or additional healthy foods. Women may choose to add another dairy serving daily to increase calcium.

ABOUT THE MENUS

The listed menus in Part III, the 30-Day Menu Plan, provide selections to choose from in a daily 2,200-calorie eating plan. The menu is a guide to help you make choices in planning, shopping, and eating. You will suffer from a poor daily diet when your meals are on a catch-as-catch-can basis. A little simple planning in your menus will result in more energy to meet the daily tasks you face.

The daily menu is broken down to eating meals at least six times a day. Just as your car can't go anywhere without gas, neither can you stay healthy and active if you skip breakfast or any other meal. As you gain more energy and become more active with this daily menu, you will find that will burn more calories than when you do not put fuel into your body.

Substitutions may be made with many foods. A good example is with fruits. I offer a wide selection of fruits on the menu. However, the season, quality, availability, and price can change the daily offering. The main point to keep in mind with any menu is to make changes from meal to meal and day to day. Eating apples for thirty days in a row is going to be boring!

Once you get used to the various food groups, you can then change foods within the same grouping. For example, you can make a substitution in the bread group to allow for your daily recommended servings of grains, breads, and cereals, or substitute one entree for another. However, this does not allow for exchanging a fruit for a second plate of pasta. Be sure to use the nutritional analysis to help you select foods that have similar caloric and nutritional content.

One of the most important things I considered in creating the daily plan is to keep the meals exciting. Vary the textures, flavors, and seasonings to keep each meal appealing. Boredom in any menu is a downfall to good eating.

Finally, remember to keep it simple. You may begin to change your good eating habits when you get too busy. I was a great example of that. I gained over 45 pounds when I became too busy to eat the right foods at the right time. This sneaks up on you very easily! After traveling and missing many regular meal times, I would eat very late at night, then go right to sleep. Today there are many excellent prepared foods readily available in supermarkets. If you do not have time to cook, that doesn't mean there is not time to plan ahead for meals on the run (See Chapter 2, What Is Healthy Food?).

So, get out a pencil right now and plan your weekly shopping list using the outline of the menu suggestions beginning on page 192. Make changes to each daily menu to fit your own active lifestyle and preferred tastes.

Adjust the foods you buy according to the seasons of the year. This does not only apply to fruits and vegetables. Your eating styles will change with the seasons as well. In the warmer months, most people desire lighter meats and seafood; in cooler weather, warmer comfort foods become appealing. Comfort foods such as soups, stews, and roasts are acceptable. However, use caution with respect to the cooking styles and how the gravies, sauces, and casseroles are prepared. Avoid using creams, butter, and fats. In my recipes and the menu plan, I offer you alternate ways of preparing these foods.

Also, as colder weather approaches, avoid the cocooning affect it brings. Do not hibernate in front of the television. No matter what physical limitations you encounter, the human body requires movement. This needs to be approached on an individual basis. Consult your physician, a personal trainer, and a registered dietitian to determine the physical activity and eating quantities that are right for you. Even with my weight loss, it took months before I had my food consumption in line with the amount of physical activity I was participating in.

Finally, keep the recipes exciting by zesting them up with chilies (hot peppers), hot sauces, vinegars, spices, herbs, or one of my favorites— caramelized garlic (See recipe, p. 104)!

Menu Substitutions

Approach each menu and recipe as a guide. Make personal choices and preferences by changing vegetables and fruits by seasonal availability and, of course, by your own individual tastes. The same guideline can be used for meats, chicken, or fish. A good number of the recipes offer substitutions such as turkey for chicken, salmon for tuna, and so on. The most important things to keep in mind are to maximize the flavors with seasonings and to enjoy the variety of textures of foods. The recipes in *Living It Up!* will provide you with the understanding you need to adapt and make these changes not just for thirty days—but for life.

Results in 30 Days

Results are determined by you—your passion, dedication, and motivation. Eating the right foods and the right amount of foods at the right time of the day will deliver the most effective results. Foods you eat can enhance your concentration in school and work and provide you with additional energy to get up and go. This increase in energy naturally leads to increased motivation to apply to physical activities and a healthy fitness routine. The results range from burning more calories, shedding some extra pounds, and keeping fit to sharpening alertness and decreasing stress.

WHAT TO DO AFTER THE 30 DAYS

Think of your first 30 days as the training camp for a lifetime of healthy, active eating. After these 30 days are up, make substitutions by using the 30-day menu guide. Make your substitutions according to your food preferences and the amount of activity for your lifestyle.

Daily Motivation Quotes

This plan also includes daily motivational, fitness, and nutrition tips to guide you along and provide you with bits of healthy information. These tips will help you begin each day, especially if you need a little extra push to get started or to keep you on track.

INTRODUCTION

Sometimes I think I was named after Curious George. I've always been particularly curious and interested in how things work, and I regularly find myself in a classroom of some form or another, seeking how-to opportunities. My first and favorite experience in the classroom of curiosity was in the kitchen. I guess I subconsciously knew this would be my professional arena, in the culinary classroom of how-to on national television.

Cooking for me is not just a passion, but a flavorful way of life. I simply cannot remember a time when I was not interested in preparing, cooking, and creating with food. At three years old I recall waking up early in the morning and sneaking into the kitchen to prepare breakfast for my family. What were my parents to do? They would become quite concerned with me climbing about the kitchen, especially considering the hazards found in the kitchen. However, they would keep an eye and ear to the kitchen, watching and listen for my early risings while admiring my young determination and craftiness.

In my house, food and meal times were a major part of family life, much as dinner time typically was for families in the 1950s and 1960s. Meals and dinner time gave my family the time around the table to share anecdotes, nostalgic reminisces, daily happenings, and interesting (and, most often, curious) activities of the day. The stories at times ranged from simple to scientific, from sometimes mild to incredibly adventurous; always, however, the catalyst of bringing my family together in this daily ritual was the food and the table.

Back in the 1970s, cooking as a profession in the U.S. wasn't the most popular career aspiration of the average high school graduate, so there simply weren't many culinary universities for me to choose from. After working for a few years in food service, I visited a close friend who was attending the Culinary Institute of America (CIA), often called the Harvard of culinary schools. There I knew I would be exposed to food as art, food as science—food as a livelihood. I knew I *had* to enroll and graduate from this finest culinary school in the world. The decision to enroll at the CIA was a milestone in my career. The CIA in the late 1970s and 1980s was the single most influential credential of the American chef. Today, more high school graduates aspire to master the culinary arts and, luckily, there are now hundreds of very highly accredited culinary programs throughout the country that train hundreds of incredibly talented chefs every year.

Years ago, chefs did not grace magazine covers or host their own television programs. This has also undergone an incredible evolution. With specialty magazines and cable television, chefs are regarded today as quality, credible "info-tainers."

After graduation from the CIA, I worked in various positions in hotel and restaurant kitchens. My first and most influential position was as the executive corporate chef to the chairman of the board of the Grumman Corporation. This position was also my most challenging. My previous experience had included developing healthy menus for perhaps one or two recipes on a menu. This was very typical of the time. At Grumman, however, the menus in the executive dining room rotated daily, on each course, with several selections for each course. Here was the challenge: every menu choice had to be a healthy, exciting dish. Most of the time, the guests were not even aware they were eating healthy foods. The best minds in the world would visit our dining room—some of the most influential people of various countries and the defense industry. It was my job to prepare for them flavorful foods, from appetizers to desserts, without the stigma of eating "healthy."

My energy level during this period was through the roof. Not only did I work over twelve hours a day, but there was a new responsibility added to my job description—training all the employees in the kitchens where I worked. Seeing a dishwasher learning the basics of cooking and progressing to become a cook and eventually run his own kitchen brought me great satisfaction. It reminded me of my own progression and growth as a chef. This training of aspiring cooks in my own kitchens segued me to adjunct teaching at a local private college culinary arts program.

After several years of part-time teaching, there was an explosion of interest in prospective students who wanted to become chefs. The economy in the U.S. was strong, and it created a great job market in the hospitality industry. The college culinary program was also growing, and I was made part of this expansion by heading up the program as the director of the Culinary Arts School. I recruited an excellent group of chef instructors and related support staff in the largest expansion of a college-level culinary program in the Long Island, New York, area. Courses we developed went well beyond just cooking. Nutrition, menu development, and management, were also part of the curriculum added to fully complement cooking classes in everything from American cuisine, international cooking, and ice carving to advanced pastry courses.

There is great satisfaction in seeing students develop their passion of learning to cook to becoming in very high demand in the culinary world. I still receive letters and e-mails from former students who have gone on to great positions all around the country. I'm incredibly proud when, in the most unlikely places around the country, I find my former students as owners of their own restaurants and heading up very impressive establishments.

But the amount of time that I was spending in the kitchen had become part-time. Most of my time at the school was spent in administration. Other student functions kept me from my first passion, cooking. After seven years I decided that it was time to move on, get back in the kitchen full-time, and open up my own restaurant. At times, everyone has a fantasy of running their own restaurant. I can remember on more than one occasion my father telling us kids at the dinner table after my mother had prepared a great dinner, "Polly, I am going to open up a restaurant." She knew better, though, because my father knew only one thing about the kitchen—that is, where his meals came from.

In some ways, my father got his wish. I opened a restaurant with my partner—and my father, who had just retired. I like to think the restaurant was a hit because of the food. However, in some warm way, we knew it was due to his ever-present smile and the calming effect he had on the staff during peak times and moments of crisis (it seems the restaurant business has at least one crisis an hour). I probably received more compliments about my father than any other employee who worked in the dining room.

He was the best partner, business associate, confident, and friend anyone could have. I guess he also got his dream, and the food always came out in time for his own meal.

As a chef-restauranteur, I learned about the unending amount of routine daily tasks and chores, from planning and purchasing to promoting, that were required. At times, we were just as busy ice carving and working at hunger benefits and festivals of every type from wine and beer-tasting dinners, as we were serving lunches and dinners at the restaurant. My visibility as a chef on Long Island, New York, offered me an opportunity to host a weekly cooking program on News12 Long Island. This was my training ground that led to a national audience on public television. My varied background in food also led to writing several books on various unique approaches in cooking.

But my background in business, marketing, television production, nutrition, and physical training is secondary to my role as a cook. As a cook, I offer an opportunity to make people smile—to make them happy to delight in tasty and nourishing foods that will provide energy and enjoyment in living. I always enjoyed sports and physical activities, but what I have learned a few short years ago is the importance fitness and proper eating plays in our daily lives. Cooking and eating the proper foods is very basic and goes hand in hand with keeping a healthy, active lifestyle.

During the past few years I've been developing a training routine that I find interesting and exciting, and which fits my daily schedule. The sport I've claimed a passion for is karate. Martial arts is an incredibly physical and mentally demanding sport. When the day came for my black belt test, I was well-prepared and anxious to face the eight-hour test head on. This test is proof of not only physical ability, but strength in spirit as well. Fortunately, my daily training and eating program gave me the energy required to maintain a strong display of metal and physical skill. My determination and spirit in my training as a chef is also carried over to my other activities.

I began as a young child with curiosity in the kitchen and a passion for cooking. With that passion I learned the need for proper eating and fitness training. Today, I share with my worldwide audience on my television programs, and Internet programs,—all new subjects for healthy, active living. My favorite recipe begins with one part proper eating; add one part daily fitness. Allow this recipe to bloom into a wonderful plan for Living It Up! If I can do it, *you* can do it!

My best wishes for healthy, active living,
George

PART I:

LEARNING TO
LIVE IT UP!

CHAPTER 1

LIVING IT UP!
"THE PLAN"

Take one look at most magazine covers, talk shows, and even best-selling books. What do you find? They all promise to have the miracle answer to help you lose weight and look and feel younger! If it was only that simple. There are no shortcuts, but there is an enjoyable way to approach good eating and healthy, active living—and it is all laid out for you in this book.

How The Plan Came About

I have found one of the most important things in trying to feel physically and mentally better is to look deep inside and know where your own strengths and weaknesses lie. Some of you may have a weakness for desserts or fatty rich foods, but for me it was eating the wrong foods at the wrong time and not getting enough of the proper exercise. Once you

pinpoint your weakness(es), you can then make modifications to reinforce your strengths so you can get yourself on the road to healthy, active living.

For example, my weakness lay in distractions. I would become very involved in my daily routine and then did not eat on any particular schedule. Using my strength in having a disciplined work ethic, I began to apply that to my weakness of not eating and exercising on schedule. This basic principle of strength conquering weakness is simple to institute once you know the basics of how it can be applied to your own life.

If you determine your weakness is eating too many fatty or sweet foods or becoming part of the furniture by sitting too much, then you have already achieved half the battle. Use your strengths—gardening, sports, singing, or another activity you enjoy—to compensate for the weakness. Use these talents to institute the changes necessary to develop a proper eating and exercise plan. Having strength in any personal trait or activity is the vehicle that will take you past any obstacle.

I was also very surprised to find that my energy level increased with eating the right foods at the right time of day. Equally important was a scheduled fitness routine. The body is a machine and, like any machine, it requires fuel to run efficiently. Simply put, without the right kind of fuel we slow down and lose momentum. Properly fueled up with the right foods at the right time of day, you will have energy to keep up with all daily activities. Other benefits, besides looking and feeling better, include the ability to actually get more work accomplished in less time. So you see, there is no downside to this plan. Just think of getting to the point where you actually enjoy exercising.

The Mindset

It's easy, once you know and understand how to get to this point. For many years I ran, biked, or participated in some type of fitness routine. But this happened every other day, or with no planned schedule. Once I made up my mind that I would no longer face a daily grind of "I did my workout," things changed. The first change was a mindset. I planned my daily menu to coincide with the fitness routine for that day. Immediately I felt the benefits: increased energy, stronger physical and mental abilities, and greater health and well-being—plus, I looked and felt great!

Reaping the Benefits of a Healthy Active Life

Like me, you can begin your fitness program with just a 20-minute walk outside—even in December! Fresh air and a time to clear your mind from all the daily responsibilities is one immediate reward.

This simple routine had the added benefit of helping me lose the first two to three pounds. The secret of the *Living It Up!* plan lies not within any headline diet or fitness machine but in a combined lifestyle plan of food and exercise. I found my energy increased each and every day, as did my attitude, when it was time to do my physical activity. It was over one year before I lost the entire 45 pounds, but it did not matter. It was five pounds at a time. That is all I ever used as a goal and that's why the plan works, because there is no pressure. You will be integrating simple lifestyle changes that will benefit you in so many ways that you will be naturally motivated to continue.

There Is a Way
MAKING THE LIVING IT UP! PLAN WORK FOR YOU

SETTING GOALS

The best way to begin is by making simple changes in your life that are easy to live with. For example, the next time you get into your car, don't drive away immediately. Just stop for a moment. You apparently have a plan and a goal to fulfill. Maybe you're about to drive to work, go shopping, or run some errands. Congratulations! The key here is to recognize the relative ease of goal-setting and to think about using this same skill that you use to execute hundreds of goals a day: some big, some small, some that require deliberate planning, some that you plan subconsciously to set conscious, life-changing ones. Start small. Don't set goals that are too ambitious or overwhelming because these are the kinds of goals you tend to abandon relatively quickly.

One of the most important goals you will ever set out to make concerns your health. Your body is your own individual, custom-made vehicle designed to take you through every journey in your life. So why not begin right now and chose a goal that will tune up your body so it can be the healthiest, most active vehicle for you? Let's begin so that by this time tomorrow, you will have already taken the first positive step.

AN EASY APPROACH TO GOAL SETTING

1. SETTING YOUR GOAL. Breaking down your objectives into individual steps is a fundamental part of the goal-setting process. This will create an aesthetic image that you'll find practical and doable—not overwhelming and extraordinary. For me, my original goal was not to lose 45 pounds. Initially, I just wanted to find a way to improve my wellness; I wanted to wake up in the morning with a burst of energy. I thought that losing five to ten pounds and keeping it off would be great. That was to be my first step. *What is yours?* Now is the time to start thinking about it.

2. GETTING ORGANIZED. Look at how you eat, how much you eat, and when you eat. Being a professional chef meant that I was constantly surrounded by food—preparing food, selecting food, planning meals, tasting new recipes, and so on. In the past, I never really overate, but since my eating schedule was haphazard and untraditional, this had to be addressed first. So, I broke down my meal schedule into a more organized menu format. Instead of the traditional three filling meals a day, I scheduled five to six smaller meals a day, which worked for me since I needed energy throughout the day and didn't always have the time to sit down to a leisurely meal. At first, eating this way seemed like too much food for me. However, after about a week, my appetite became conditioned to this approach. Finding and adhering to a style-of-eating plan that fits your life will help you maintain an energy level that will ultimately motivate you to exercise and be more active. This step will put you on the road to a more healthy, active lifestyle, and you will have more pep in your step and zip in your doo-dah!

3. ENLISTING FAMILY AND FRIENDS. Sometimes working alone can be frustrating, uncreative, and, unfortunately, boring. Working in a team, however, can give you a natural, satisfying sense of belonging and approval. Enlisting family and friends in your plans is invaluable because it gives you an unconditional support system, with devoted cheerleaders and coaches on the sidelines. Without this motivational lifeline, it is easier for redundancy to prevail. Introducing and sharing your excitement and progress with others is overwhelmingly uplifting. Having a buddy to exercise with or a pal to share new healthy recipes with intensifies the sense of comradery that is the essence of successful teamwork! So don't go about it alone. Share your knowledge and spirit with others, it will come back to you tenfold.

After losing some of my initial weight and increasing my energy, I enrolled in a martial arts class, in anticipation of my daughter joining by my example. Not only did I further improve my own body, but this positive fitness activity proved contagious to my family and friends. Now at sixteen, my daughter is preparing for her black belt. Other family and friends have joined martial arts programs and fitness centers and walk the dog with a little more pep.

4. DON'T GET FRUSTRATED IF YOU SLIP. Each day is a vibrant, new day to exercise proper eating. But even with a winning team of supporters, you can lose a game or two. There may be days when your schedule goes awry and your meal schedule is off, and you subsequently lose synch in the ol' energy department. Don't let it get you down. When your energy fizzles, turn it around. Make yourself even *more* determined to work harder and not to let it happen again. Basically, don't be disappointed in yourself if you slip—just move forward eagerly! The key is to get back on track immediately. Do not put it off until later. Do it *now!*

Remember to take pride in absolutely every stage of progress, no matter how small. To reach the summit of the mountain inevitably takes one step at a time.

5. REWARD YOURSELF. Appreciate your successes, no matter how small, and reward yourself with nonfood items. I remember my clothes did not fit well after losing a few pounds, so one great self-reward was to treat myself to new, stylish clothing. Simply creating the plan, being dedicated, and accomplishing your goals entitles you to a reward. Make it an active celebration—you deserve it!

SIMPLIFY YOUR LIFE

Okay, you now have the basics of goal setting. But in order to put them to use you'll need to know more, so let's begin with lifestyle changes. It's time to stop and smell the roses.

One of the most valuable lessons I have learned was not from a textbook or in a school classroom. It was presented by my father who said to me during all the hustle and bustle of life in the 1990s, "George, you must stop and smell the roses." Sure, this sounds like a simple thing to do, right? Well, let me tell you—it is more difficult than it appears. It requires time, patience, and interpretation. Today's hectic lifestyle makes it even more difficult to appreciate the little things—those things we tend to take for granted, like the sweet scent of a rose.

Oftentimes, we learn from children. The same rose that may have been overlooked several times by an adult distracted by unending demands may actually have been enjoyed by a four- or five-year-old over and over again. Before you know it, the short life of that rose may approach its end, and you may never again get the chance to experience its gift. Remember, it's okay to regress a bit, to act like a four- or five-year-old, to put down the newspaper, pick up the rose, and give it a nice deep sniff! Just as it is important to appreciate the small wonders of the world, it is just as important not to dwell on the small blunders of the world. Each day you will always face challenges at home, work, and in social situations that will pass as quickly as they come upon us. During any trying times, it is even more important to keep a proper eating plan and fitness routine. Instead of letting anything tear you up inside, head for the gym or even out for a long walk. You will be amazed to find, once you step back, that the difficulty you faced was not all that big.

When I finally took the time—and my father's advice—I genuinely understood what it meant to appreciate the little things in life. The next time you walk by the garden, stop and smell the roses. You will notice others stopping to smell them with you—it's contagious! And thanks, Dad!

IDENTIFYING YOUR FOOD STRENGTHS AND WEAKNESSES

The dinner plates have just been cleared off the table and now the waiter places the scrumptious, tantalizing dessert tray in front of you. Do you:

A) smile and say, "No, thank you"
B) order something to split with your dinner guest
C) order a dessert for you and your guest and eat them both

If you answer C, it's safe to say that sweets are your weakness. If you answer B, you're on the right track. And if A is your answer, congratulations! You're getting the idea.

Weaknesses come in a variety of forms—you may give in to sweets, you may religiously supersize the meal deal, you may be compelled to finish the bread basket, or you may indulge in crunchy, fried foods. Whatever it is, it is important to identify your weakness(es) and pinpoint exactly when you tend to falter. Once you have accepted the fact that you have a weakness and can identify when you're more susceptible, you can more easily modify your positive eating plan.

But just as it is essential to understand what your weak points are, it is even more important to identify your strengths. A healthy positive attitude is better for you than a healthy portion of fried calamari or a gooey dessert. Being confident and proud of yourself and being mindful of achieving your goal toward an active healthy life style is a powerful driving force that enables us to move past our deficiencies and overcome temptation. Positive mental attitude, confidence and pride should be the main ingredients in the recipe of life.

For example, I know one of my more noteworthy strengths is my keen ability to plan, whereas my weakness tends to be how easily I can become preoccupied and enveloped with projects and chores. Because of this weakness, I can easily be thrown off schedule and end up having dinner at 10:30 P.M. After pinpointing this weakness, I now make a deliberate and conscious effort to plan my menus and eat on a regular time schedule. The same can be said for maintaining my fitness schedule. Before evaluating my strengths and weaknesses, I would get so wrapped up in work that my exercise schedule was easily overlooked and frequently bypassed. Not today. Now I consciously make an effort to plan my exercise schedule and stick to it!

If your weakness is desserts, you must compensate by relying on your strengths. Allow your strength to overpower the weakness by focusing on what comes naturally to you. Believe in yourself, that you are much more powerful than any weakness. It may be difficult, but once you pinpoint your particular weakness, you will begin to develop stronger self-esteem and that will lead to other types of success. Remember, strengths are strong, but weakness are just that—weak.

Each day you encounter many challenges that require determination and willpower. The big challenges will be overcome after the small challenges are met. Being disciplined by taking a walk, running, or participating in any fitness routine will lead to developing and achieving that nonquitting spirit. As you maintain a regular schedule and inevitably increase your self-confidence, you will find it easier to pass on the scrumptuous desserts or the crunchy fried foods. Every small accomplishment provides the increased willpower needed to face life's challenges head-on!

There may be a day when you wind up in a confrontation, and you give in to your weakness. If you go off track, remember losing one battle does not mean you will lose the war. Do not lose hope. Have confidence in yourself and, instead, adopt a nonquitting spirit and execute it every step of the way.

CHAPTER 2

WHAT IS HEALTHY FOOD?

When many people see or hear the word *healthy*, their brains shut down. The reason is that they think healthy food is either going to taste like cardboard or going to leave you craving for more. But suppose healthy food could be tasty food, even without salt, or butter, or sugar? Taste and flavor are not derived wholly from the ingredients, but by how foods are prepared, their texture, accompaniments, and much more.

Foods and cooking have changed drastically over the past ten years. Years ago, meals were fattier, heavier, richer, and more abundant. As a young cook, I remember preparing a 16-ounce New York strip or loin steak, seasoning the unmarinated meat with just salt and pepper, soaking the meat in a pan of oil, grilling it to order, and then plating it with a pat of butter.

These days, most people are more conscious of what they eat and how much they eat. The recommended portion size today is a surprisingly satisfying five- to six-ounce steak, served with flavorful, bulkier accompaniments. For the preparation, instead of using salt and pepper, we marinate the steak overnight or apply a dry seasoning rub that consists of a combination of spices and herbs such as paprika, powdered garlic, thyme, oregano, and crushed black peppercorns. The steak is then grilled with no additional oil. The finished steak is topped with its natural juices or a variety of salsas, and served with savory high-fiber vegetables and salad greens. Clearly, we have reduced much fat this way, yet we can enjoy an even tastier, varied meal with exciting texture.

So, healthy does not mean having to "eat like a bird" or going hungry. Rather, healthy refers more to moderation of certain foods while consuming mostly foods that will provide the essential vitamins, minerals, and basic fuels for your body to operate more efficiently.

Healthy Seasonings

You know that grilling foods instead of panfrying them eliminates extra fat, but what do you know about healthy seasonings? Over the years I have discovered that many people do not have enough experience in using seasonings to make their foods flavorful. An interesting fact to remember is that it's the amount of flavor, not the amount of food, that satisfies the palate. When the taste buds are not enticed or excited with seasonings and flavorings, you can easily become bored and crave fattier, saltier, and sweeter foods.

Because most herbs and spices are natural, it should be just as natural for you to learn to incorporate healthy seasonings into your recipes for healthy, active living. Start by becoming familiar with different spices and herbs. Seasoning is not just using salt and pepper! Salt is not a seasoning but rather a stimulant to the taste buds. Your taste buds become easily accustomed to the effect of salt. But your taste buds can also learn to like many other exciting flavors that you simply are not using.

I will not discuss the negative medical effects of having too much salt in your diet, but what I will highlight is all the great flavors to be gained by using chilies, cumin, curries, and peppers. My favorite herbs include fresh basil, rosemary, thyme, and sage. In addition to the many spices and herbs in my recipes, I also include flavorings as well. Common flavorings I use are vinegars, citrus, mustards, garlic, ginger, and fruit juices. I'm sure you will like them as much as I do. I hope that they will help you to experiment more and come up with your own exciting flavor combinations.

Satisfying Texture

To satisfy the texture component of healthy, active eating, you may add crunch and zip to a dish with nuts, seeds, and even horseradish. To wake up a sleepy recipe, you can learn to master the use of texture and apply it to your cooking. When you were young, your first foods were soft and bland. Now that your palate is mature and strong, you can indulge in hot, tangy, and crunchy foods. Many foods with satisfying texture are those that are high in fiber and bulk, and know that a diet high in fiber and bulk can decrease the risk of certain types of cancer and type II diabetes. This food also fills you up—not out!

After a little practice and experimentation, with basic seasonings and marinades as flavor enhancers, you will soon discover an entirely new, exciting world of healthy eating.

Keeping Fit and Having Fun

Finding time for a good fitness routine in your schedule can sometimes be a workout in itself. But an active fitness routine is as necessary for balanced health and well-being as eating and sleeping. Naturally, you should seek the advice of your doctor before beginning any form of physical activity. Together, you and your doctor can create a program that will help you reach your fitness goal and is suitable for your ability level.

THE SECRET OF MOTIVATION

First, you must get motivated. Once you understand and value the benefits of a healthy, active lifestyle, don't dwell on losing weight. Instead, focus on eating for health, feeling good, and performing better physically. Keep in mind that the *process is more important than the result.* Remember that exercising and eating right gives you health and fitness benefits as well as weight loss. If you focus on making healthy lifestyle changes, the pounds and inches will take care of themselves.

Only when you do this will you be able to initiate a creative, interesting fitness routine. There are so many types of fitness regimes from which you can choose. Some people like yoga, some people like kickboxing. Choose what interests you, but whatever it is, think of it as fun, and not a chore. Positive mental attitude is pivotal for successfully adopting a healthy fitness plan. A professional physical trainer can help adapt and modify your program to avoid boredom. Varying exercises in your daily routine will also help you work out different muscle groups while allowing other groups to rest. On some days you may train with a cardio routine such as running or speed walking, while other days you can do strength training with light weights. The combinations are endless.

Remember to allow for a slow, but steady, increase in stamina and endurance; do not expect miracles. Measure progress over a period of time. Effective results are progressive results. Initially you may see more noticeable, superficial results in the first couple of months; after a while, the progress may not be as apparent. Realize, however, that the results achieved are deeper—in the development of your strength in controling your lifestyle—by then.

THE IMPORTANCE OF HAVING FUN

One of the best ways to keep up with any program is by doing the activity with other people. Join a team, gym, or martial arts class. Motivation is critical in any fitness program, and a group can provide a valuable support system, especially on the days that you just don't have the get-up-and-go. Having this support system may also make the difference in not just doing an activity, but in having fun doing it as well.

Having fun is what it's all about. The old saying, "No pain, no gain" may be true in competitive sports. However, keeping up with a consistent fitness routine involves enjoying what you are doing. And, believe me, avoiding pain is much more comfortable than overdoing it. A healthy burn in your abs means you are working the muscles, but a painful feeling or lingering body aches from overexertion may eventually act as a deterrent.

All forms of activity—from walking on nature paths or city streets to rowing, biking, horseback riding, or martial arts training—count. The main thing is doing what your body will allow and doing what you enjoy. Sitting on a couch with the remote control in hand doesn't count—unless, of course, you are watching one of my programs!

Water

How much water do you need when participating in an active physical fitness program that includes running, biking, swimming, or other cardiosports? According to the American Society of Sports Trainers the recommended amount is to drink at least a pint of water within one hour before a workout, eight ounces every half-hour during a workout, and one pint immediately after a workout.

The recipe is very simple: two parts hydrogen and one part oxygen. However, there is so much drinking water available that making it is not even a consideration. Water is taken so much for granted, and it is surprising how few people actually consume enough. Consider that the adult body is made up of more than 50 percent water, and our bones are composed of 20 percent!

The average adult should consume at least eight to ten glasses of water a day. On days when I'm resting—not working out or exercising—I will drink well over ten glasses. During heavy workout days, I will replace lost water by drinking about ten glasses within two hours after a workout. Day-to-day requirements change for all of us in accordance with hot weather, exercise routines, and health considerations.

Water helps in digestion; it also gives a healthy glow to the skin, lubricates joints, controls body temperature, and protects tissue. It also transports nutrients to the organ tissue and waste out of the body. You need an adequate amount of water to live—period.

WATER TIPS

- Drink 8 to 10 eight-ounce glasses of water each day. If you wait until you're thirsty, you're already dehydrated!
- Freeze bottled water to keep it cold and use it as an ice pack. As the bottled water begins to melt, you'll have plenty of drinking water.
- Drink water out of your favorite water bottle. Be sure your favorite water bottle is always handy and filled with water.
- Keep extra water bottles handy—in your car, at your desk, and around the house. You'll be surprised at how much more water you will consume.
- Drink a glass of water 30 minutes before a meal, and you will not be as hungry when you sit down to eat. The stomach signals the brain 20 minutes after it has received food or liquids.
- I prefer to drink water at room temperature to avoid stomach cramping, especially before, during, and immediately after a workout.
- Prevent dehydration by drinking water before any physical activ-

ity, not just during and after. Increase water consumption in warm weather and during times when perspiring.

- Drink an additional glass of water per every cup of coffee, soda, or other caffeinated beverage you consume. Caffeine is a diuretic that will rob your body of water that must be replaced.

SPORTS DRINKS

Sports drinks are not a replacement for water, but they do offer assistance in rehydration and replace electrolytes that are lost during intense workouts. Most are made with a high fructose corn syrup base and provide a quick energy boost that lasts only a short period of time. Unfortunately, too many aspiring athletes substitute sports drinks for proper eating and drinking plain water. Another downside is that after spending 20 minutes on a treadmill or other physical activity, a sweetened sports drink can add on the calories you just burned off—or maybe even more!

Learn To Eat Properly

Eat five to six planned meals a day to avoid the impulse to overeat or to eat the wrong foods. Simply put, your stomach is a body clock. Proper eating habits require keeping track of time to maintain high energy levels and restrict impulse eating. Skipping a meal to keep from overeating will only cause you to eat more later on. You may think you are cutting back on calories, but before you even realize, by the middle of the day, you're giving in to impulse eating. Diving into snacks, consuming fast food, or doubling up on portions at the next mealtime will be the only result.

DON'T SHOP WHEN YOU'RE HUNGRY

Food shopping on an empty stomach will result in extra food in your cart. After all, how could you not put extra items in your cart? The aroma of breads baking and foods cooking in the store will be hypnotic. That's why it's best to shop after eating and with a shopping list in hand to avoid hunger shopping. And it's not rude to say, "No, thank you," to the friendly servers parked at the end of the aisles armed with toothpicks and beverage napkins for you to sample the food's they've prepared.

Nowadays, the choices while eating out or grabbing a meal to go couldn't be better. Supermarkets have prepared meals; local restaurants provide healthy, wholesome, and exciting food choices. Choices range from pita wraps, roasted chickens, sushi, soups, and entire meals. When making your selections, you can often find a nutrition label that can aid you in your selection of lower fat fare.

But even though the choices are better today, you still have to plan on how you will be incorporating prepared foods into your active, healthy lifestyle. My general rule is: if you need to speak into a microphone to order your food, then your daily diet is in trouble. A meal decision on the run can be trouble if plans have not been made in advance, so here are some tips that should help.

AVOID FAST FOOD. A quick drive-thru for the super burger will be approximately one-third of your daily calorie allowance and *two* days of fat allowance. I know I would prefer to eat a lot more bulky food than one fatty burger. Food high in fiber is actually more satisfying and gives me a much more even flow of energy to do all the activities in my daily schedule.

PLAN MEALS AHEAD. Not all food needs to be picked up in the hot food sectionof your grocery store; try looking in the freezer section. There are many great choices of fully prepared entrees and individual dishes in the freezer section. Just make sure you read the label. Combine a frozen entree with a salad and fresh fruit. This will permit you to have a serving of sorbet, fat free ice cream, or lowfat cookies. You now have a great menu for the catch-as-catch-can days.

CHOOSE CAREFULLY FROM A MENU. When eating out in restaurants, you need to look over the menu choices carefully. Just because the menu item sounds healthy does not automatically make it so. Ask the server specifics on the offerings so you can be guided to better selections. Watch out for healthy salads that are served with a large portion of dressing. Ask to have all sauces and dressings served on the side, even if they are low fat. A low fat food item can still be high in calories, with higher sugar content to replace the flavor lost in fat.

DON'T EAT THE BUTTER. When the bread basket arrives, stay clear of the butter. Do not assume that because the bread is dark it is whole wheat. A better choice is to eat the breadsticks, whole grain bread, or French bread. Eat in moderation. Remember that the bread usually arrives prior to the salad and other bulky satisfying foods.

IF YOU REALLY WANT DESSERT. . . . Don't order dessert from the same restaurant in which you have just eaten your meal. Instead, get up, move around, and allow the meal to satisfy you. Remember that it takes 20 or more minutes for the brain to realize the stomach is full! Eat dessert later; then, choose fresh fruit, sorbet, or a couple of fat free cookies.

TRY THE DAILY SPECIAL. I find this selection is usually easier to adapt to a healthy choice.

EAT ACCORDING TO THE CLOCK. If you're having a late meal, choose lighter foods on the menu.

DON'T EAT OUT WHEN YOU ARE STARVING. Dining out is a lot like shopping. If you have skipped meals, you will tend to order more food than you need to, or will dive into the bread basket. This is when your eyes are bigger than your stomach. But the amount of food you order when eating out should not be the only consideration. The cooking methods used by the restaurants must be taken into consideration. Unlike eating at home, you are eating foods that you have not seen prepared. It's okay to ask the waitperson questions about ingredients and how the dish is prepared. The size of the portions is also important. Usually, you will receive a far larger portion than you need to or are able to comfortably eat. That's good news—but only if you take the leftovers home. Unlimited servings are what buffets are all about. Buffets are very enticing and can offer numerous good choices such as salads, fruits, and vegetables. Now is when you need to exercise your self-control with a smaller sampling of meats and starches to round out your meal. I have always valued a nonquitting spirit, but in this case you need to know when to quit!

TIPS FOR STAYING ON TRACK

Most meals will be consumed at home. But there are lots of eating traps at home to avoid. The following will help you stay on track.

- Avoid eating out of the box, bag, or wrapper. Measure what you eat either with a scale or visually on a plate. Eating out of a package is the ultimate in impulse eating. Just don't do it!
- Avoid plating meals at the table. Plate meals in the kitchen and bring them to the table. This helps to avoid the temptation for seconds.
- Avoid refined sugar. Use unprocessed forms such as honey, molasses, natural fruit juices, and cane and corn syrups.
- Avoid refined flours. Use products made from whole wheat, whole grain, oats, and oat bran.
- Avoid eating at your desk, in front of the fridge, and in the car. Eating at the table is more comfortable and allows you to focus on foods, flavors, and fulfillment.
- Avoid food "triggers" such as fatty, sugary, and salty snacks. If your brain says, "I'll only eat just one," chances are you shouldn't eat any.
- Avoid letting yourself get too hungry. The five to six meals a day plan in this book will satisfy your active appetite.
- Avoid stress. Most of us eat more during times of anxiety. This is when you can use relaxation techniques such as meditation or yoga.
- Avoid picking or sampling! It's too easy to forget the amount of food you've eaten or picked on when measuring serving sizes. Picking gives you a false reading and an underestimation of the amount of food you've actually consumed.
- Avoid distractions at mealtime such as the television, telephone, or newspapers; enjoy the TV, telephone, and newspapers without the distraction of foods.

YOUR "SPRING TRAINING." Each year during spring training, baseball teams start from the basics, regardless of the results of the previous season. They look back to correct their weaknesses and enhance their strengths. Today is the first day of your spring training. Pinpoint your weaknesses, celebrate your strengths. Apply positive mental attitudes and have a nonquitting spirit. Get organized and have a plan—and stick to it! Results are inevitable.

Strive for a healthy life and wellness for yourself, your family, and your friends. When you get back to basics and beyond the weaknesses of yesterday, you will begin to go forward.

In this special recipe book, I offer you recipes for active, healthy living—an eating and cooking guide for life. Approach food today as a flavorful enhancement towards an exciting tomorrow. With this all natural modification for living, you will feel better, look better, and obtain a zest for life like never before.

CHAPTER 3

STOCKING YOUR PANTRY

Here is a guide for the basic foods you need to have on hand in order to cook and eat in a healthy way. Most of these staples have a fairly long shelf life. These foods are what you need in order to prepare the recipes for the 30-day Menu Plan I have provided.

I have not listed perishables, since today there are so many ways to purchase these food items. For example, chicken breasts can be purchased frozen and thawed out quickly in the microwave, or fresh and then individually frozen, or whole chickens can be bought, cut up, and then frozen. Do what is best for your budget of time and money.

Use this checklist to go through your own pantry, refrigerator, or freezer and check off the supplies you already have. Whatever is missing is what you can buy.

SNACKS

raisins
frozen grapes
rice cakes
baked or fat free tortilla chips
low fat graham crackers

frozen bananas
fat free pretzels
popcorn
fat free cookies

GROCERY

applesauce
fat free broths
all kinds of canned beans
   (red, black, cannelli, chick
      peas, navy, pinto, white)
sesame seeds
unsalted pecans
unsalted peanuts
fat free salad dressings
   (careful—some are
      higher in sugar)
pitted ripe olives
pasta made with durham wheat
   (angel hair, penne, elbow,
      linguine, rigatoni, fettucine,
      lasagna, cavatelli)
low fat cooking spray

fat free soups
clam juice
low sugar jelly
low fat peanut butter
low fat mayonnaise
poppy seeds
unsalted walnuts
salsas (buy lower sodium choices)
solid white tuna in water
dill pickles
pitted black olives
long grain brown rice
arborio rice
tomato sauce
canned plum tomatoes
olive oil
vegetable oil or a polyunsaturated oil

BEVERAGES

bottled water
orange juice
apple juice
pineapple juice

decaffeinated teas
tomato juice
cranberry juice
grapefruit juice

BREADS

whole grain breads
low fat flour tortillas
fat free muffins
rolled oats
bran cereal

whole wheat pitas
English muffins
fortified whole grain cereals
Special K, Cheerios, shredded wheat

DAIRY

fat free milk
plain yogurt
regular margarine (for baking only)
egg substitute
feta cheese

fat free half and half
fat free sour cream
reduced or fat free margarine
fat free cheeses
fat free Cool Whip

CONDIMENTS

balsamic vinegar
honey
hot sauces
steak sauce
lite soy sauce
horseradish
corn syrup

cider vinegar
prepared mustards
barbecue sauce
sesame oil
ketchup
brown sugar

DRIED HERBS AND SPICES

allspice
black pepper
cinnamon
cumin
hot pepper flakes
Madras curry powder
nutmeg
paprika
sage

basil
cayenne pepper
coriander
garlic powder
leaf thyme
mustard powder
oregano
rosemary

PART II:

THE RECIPES

APPETIZERS , BREADS, AND BREAKFASTS

Make it small or make it mini—the kids will love it either way! Be sure to make extra for the big kids as well.

MINI PIZZA CROSTINI

Makes 4 servings
Temperature: Medium grill or 350°F oven

16 baguette bread slices, ¹/₄-inch thick
¹/₄ cup pizza or seasoned tomato sauce
¹/₂ cup low fat mozzarella cheese
1 teaspoon oregano

Preheat grill or oven to 350°F. Arrange the baguette slices on a nonstick baking pan. Top with tomato sauce, cheese, and oregano. Bake for 4 to 5 minutes, or until the bread is toasted and cheese has melted.

NUTRITIONAL INFORMATION

CALORIES 160

PROTEIN	8 g	CHOLESTEROL	24 mg
FAT	3 g	FIBER	1 g
SAT. FAT	1.5 g	SODIUM	450 mg

Focaccia is the ideal replacement for bread with dinner. It is also excellent as a sandwhich bread.

FOCACCIA

Makes 6 servings
Temperature: medium grill, then low or 400°F oven

1 pizza disc (Whole Wheat Focaccia recipe, page 28)
2 tablespoons olive oil

Preheat the grill or oven. Brush the bottom of a pie pan with 1 tablespoon of the olive oil. Flatten the dough on the pan with your fingertips or a rolling pin. Poke a few holes in the dough with a fork.

Place on the grill, then turn over after the dough turns a light brown. Brush the top with the remaining oil and place desired toppings on top. To bake in an oven, add the desired topping(s). Bake approximately 8 to 10 minutes, or until done.

The focaccia is done when a hollow sound is heard by tapping with a finger.

SUGGESTED TOPPINGS: USE ANY OR ALL

2 tablespoons caraway seeds
1 tablespoon kosher salt
2 tablespoons sesame seeds
1 tablespoon poppy seeds
2 tablespoons fresh garlic, finely chopped
2 tablespoons sundried tomatoes, plumped and chopped

NUTRITIONAL INFORMATION

CALORIES 140

PROTEIN	5 g	CHOLESTEROL	27 mg
FAT	3 g	FIBER	4 g
SAT. FAT	0 g	SODIUM	0 mg

Try to find a store that makes the mozzarella fresh. The difference will be a silky smooth cheese versus one that is stringy.

PESTO TOMATOES AND FRESH MOZZARELLA

Makes 4 servings

8 red lettuce leaves, washed and dried
3 tablespoons Pesto (see page 168)
6 plum tomatoes, split in half, or vine-ripened tomatoes sliced 1-inch thick
1/2 pound fresh mozzarella, sliced into 12 pieces
2 tablespoons balsamic vinegar
1 tablespoon olive oil
freshly ground black pepper

Arrange the red lettuce leaves on a plate. Place the tomato halves or slice-son top of the lettuce. Spread pesto on top of the tomatoes and place the mozzarella on top of the pesto. Drizzle with balsamic vinegar, olive oil, and freshly ground black pepper.

NUTRITIONAL INFORMATION

CALORIES 210

PROTEIN	14 g	CHOLESTEROL	7 mg
FAT	15 g	FIBER	1 g
SAT. FAT	6 g	SODIUM	280 mg

Dig through the refrigerator—you never know what great fillings leftovers can make. This low fat frittata is ready in ten minutes.

FRITTATA

Makes 2 servings

4 egg whites, beaten
fresh ground black pepper

FOR THE FILLING:
1 teaspoon fresh basil, chopped
1 plum tomato, chopped
¹/₄ cup cooked broccoli florets, cut into small pieces
¹/₄ cup grilled chicken, chopped
¹/₂ baked or boiled potato, chopped
2 tablespoons reduced fat cheese (Monterey Jack, cheddar, or mozzarella)
1 tablespoon olive oil

Spray an 8-inch nonstick egg or sauté pan with cooking spray. Preheat to medium temperature. Add the olive oil and tomatoes and cook for 1 minute. Add the chicken, potato, and basil. Cook until the potatoes are hot. Add the broccoli and increase the temperature to high. Add the egg whites; stir to mix. Lower the temperature to medium and cover for 2 minutes. Use a spatula to carefully flip the frittata over. Place the cheese on top and cover for 2 additional minutes. Serve hot or chill and cut into wedges and serve as an appetizer.

ADDITIONAL FILLING SUGESTIONS:

cooked chopped spinach	sliced mushrooms
asparagus	sautéed peppers
turkey	cooked sweet potatoes
shrimp	Caramelized Onions (see page 105)

NUTRITIONAL INFORMATION

CALORIES 200			
PROTEIN	16 g	CHOLESTEROL	12 mg
FAT	9 g	FIBER	2 g
SAT. FAT	1.5 g	SODIUM	310 mg

At a recent family gathering, my niece made the bruschetta. We all looked in amazement at how much she had prepared. But every last piece disappeared in minutes!

TOMATO ROAST PEPPER
BRUSCHETTA

Makes 4 servings

8 slices whole wheat multigrain French bread
4 plum tomatoes—split, deseeded, and chopped into small pieces
1 green bell pepper—split, deseeded, roasted or grilled, and chopped
6 cloves Caramelized Garlic (see page 104)
juice of one lime
2 tablespoons fresh cilantro, rough chopped
fresh ground black pepper

Mix the tomatoes, bell pepper, caramelized garlic, lime juice, cilantro, and black pepper. Cover and marinate the tomato mixture overnight or for at least one hour.

Toast the bread and then cool. Top the toasted bread with one tablespoon of the tomato topping. Serve immediately.

NUTRITIONAL INFORMATION

CALORIES 170			
PROTEIN	6 g	CHOLESTEROL	33 mg
FAT	2.5 g	FIBER	5 g
SAT. FAT	0.5 g	SODIUM	300 mg

This is a great lunch or snack to make after a hard workout because it helps replace carbs and protein.

WHOLE WHEAT PITA PIZZA

Makes 2 servings
Temperature: Medium grill or 350°F oven

2 whole wheat pocketless pitas
4 plum tomatoes, sliced thin
1/4 cup part-skim mozzarella cheese
1 tablespoon Parmesan cheese
1 teaspoon oregano
1 teaspoon basil
fresh ground black pepper

Preheat oven or grill. Arrange tomato slices on top of the pitas. Top the tomatoes with the mozzarella and Parmesan cheeses, oregano, basil, and black pepper.

Bake pitas for 5 to 8 minutes, or until the cheese is melted.

NUTRITIONAL INFORMATION

CALORIES 250

PROTEIN	12 g	CHOLESTEROL	41 mg
FAT	5 g	FIBER	6 g
SAT. FAT	2.5 g	SODIUM	480 mg

Involve the kids whenever you make a dough recipe; there's something they enjoy about flour and water that's better than any toy or game!

WHOLE WHEAT FOCACCIA

Makes 6 servings (2 focaccias)
Temperature: medium grill or 370°F oven

FOR THE DOUGH:
1¹/2 teaspoons active dry yeast
¹/4 cup warm water (between 105° and 115°)
¹/2 tablespoon honey
2¹/2 cups whole wheat flour
¹/2 cup whole grain flour
¹/2 cup bread flour
¹/4 teaspoon salt
³/4 cup warm water
1 tablespoon olive oil

Combine the yeast and ¹/4 cup warm water and stir well. Set aside for 8 to 10 minutes, or until the surface of the water begins to bubble.

Place the honey, olive oil, and salt in the remaining ³/4 cup of water. Add the yeast mixture and combine with whole wheat, bread, and whole grain flours. Mix in a large bowl for 8 minutes, or knead by hand for 10 minutes.

Place the dough in a lightly oiled bowl, cover, and place in the refrigerator overnight or for at least 6 to 8 hours.

Preheat oven or grill. Remove the dough from the refrigerator 30 minutes before using. To prepare the focaccia, spread the dough out to about 1-inch thick. Shapes can be round, oval, or rectangular. Odd shapes make it look rustic. Place the dough on a pizza pan, pizza stone, or nonstick cookie sheet. If baking on a grill, you can quickly grill right on the grates then place on top of a few heated bricks to finish baking.

Brush the dough lightly with olive oil and top with your favorite combination of toppings. Bake the focaccia for about 8 to 10 minutes or until done. The focaccia is done when a hollow sound is heard by tapping with a finger.

olive oil

Caramelized Garlic or Caramelized Onions (see pages 104–105)

plum or sundried tomatoes

green onions

olives

fresh or dried herbs: basil, cilantro, oregano, thyme, rosemary, or sage

spices: paprika, cumino, rough crushed black peppercorns, cinnamon

seeds: caraway, poppy, pumpkin, sesame

nuts: pecan, walnut, peanut

NUTRITIONAL INFORMATION

CALORIES 130

PROTEIN	5 g	CHOLESTEROL	27 mg
FAT	2 g	FIBER	4 g
SAT. FAT	0 g	SODIUM	50 mg

I have always believed in using local ingredients. There are so many varieties of crab that can be used in this recipe. If you're not using lump crabmeat, increase the amount of bread crumbs to approximately 3/4 cup.

STUFFED ARTICHOKES WITH CRAB

Makes 4 servings
Temperature: grill medium, then low, or 350° oven

4 artichokes
1/2 pound lump or Dungeness crabmeat
2 tablespoons olive oil
1/4 onion, chopped
4 cloves Caramelized Garlic (see page 104)
2 green onions, chopped
1 red bell pepper, chopped
1 rib celery, chopped
1 teaspoon thyme
1 teaspoon Tabasco
pinch nutmeg
fresh ground black pepper
1/4 cup fresh bread crumbs
2 egg whites
juice from 1 lemon
1 cup water

Preheat the grill or oven.

Preheat a sauté pan. Add the olive oil, onion, caramelized garlic, bell pepper, and celery. Sauté 2 to 3 minutes on medium, then cool. Mix in thyme, Tabasco, nutmeg, fresh ground black pepper, bread crumbs, and egg whites. Combine all the ingredients and add the crabmeat. Set aside.

Lay the artichokes on their sides. Cut off the top 1/2 inch, reach inside, and pull out the chokes (the hairy looking pieces) and discard. Fill the artichokes with the crab stuffing and put into an ovenproof pan with one cup water and the juice from one lemon. Bake for 25 to 30 minutes covered; remove the cover an additional 5 minutes to brown.

NUTRITIONAL INFORMATION

CALORIES 210			
PROTEIN	19 g	CHOLESTEROL	19 mg
FAT	8 g	FIBER	8 g
SAT. FAT	1 g	SODIUM	370 mg

They may taste nutty or sweet, but toasted sesame seeds offer a great crunch and a smile to a special diner in my life!

PHYLLO LEEKS WITH SESAME CRUST

Makes 4 servings
Temperature: medium then low grill, or 350°F oven

4 leeks, split in half and washed, then blanched in boiling water
2 tablespoons sesame seeds
8 sheets phyllo dough
2 tablespoons bread crumbs
2 tablespoons olive oil
4 tablespoons feta cheese
1 egg white
oil spray
fresh ground black pepper

Preheat oven or grill. Brush the leeks with olive oil. Lay out phyllo dough sheets one by one. Spray with oil spray, then sprinkle a small amount of bread crumbs between each layer. Repeat until there are four sheets.

Cut the phyllo into strips the length of the leeks. Top with fresh ground black pepper. Place half the leeks and cheese on top and brush with egg white. Top with sesame seeds. Repeat for remaining leeks and cheese.

Bake or grill for 25 minutes, or until golden brown.

NUTRITIONAL INFORMATION

CALORIES 280

PROTEIN	7 g	CHOLESTEROL	33 mg
FAT	13 g	FIBER	3 g
SAT. FAT	3 g	SODIUM	340 mg

Serve as a dip or spread. Either way, it's a great healthy way to snack.

HUMMUS

Serves 6

1 15-ounce can chickpeas, drained
3 cloves Caramelized Garlic (see page 104)
1 tablespoon tahini paste (optional)
1 teaspoon cumin
1 teaspoon Tabasco
juice of $^1/_2$ lemon
3 tablespoons plain lowfat yogurt

Puree chickpeas in a food processor. Add garlic, tahini, cumin, Tabasco, lemon, and yogurt. Mix all ingredients well. Allow to set for 30 minutes prior to serving.

Serve with toasted pita and raw vegetables.

Tahini is a paste made from ground sesame seeds and is a good source of zinc and calcium.

NUTRITIONAL INFORMATION

CALORIES 80

PROTEIN	3 g	CHOLESTEROL	13 mg
FAT	1.5 g	FIBER	4 g
SAT. FAT	0 g	SODIUM	160 mg

Greek foods have an excellent flavor and texture. This bruschetta celebrates the Greek heritage.

WHOLE GRAIN HONEY BRUSCHETTA

Makes 6 servings
Temperature: Grill low or 350°F oven

12 slices multigrain whole wheat dense-style bread
1/2 cup frozen chopped spinach, squeezed dry
4 tablespoons feta cheese
2 tablespoons olive oil
4 cloves Caramelized Garlic (see page 104)
1 tablespoon honey
1 teaspoon Tabasco
juice of 1 lemon
fresh ground black pepper

Brush the bread with olive oil and lightly toast. Allow to cool.

Mix the spinach, garlic, honey, Tabasco, lemon, and black pepper. Top the bread with the spinach mixture. Place the feta cheese on top of the spinach. Warm in the oven until the cheese is melted. Serve warm or cold.

NUTRITIONAL INFORMATION

CALORIES 210			
PROTEIN	7 g	CHOLESTEROL	30 mg
FAT	8 g	FIBER	4 g
SAT. FAT	2 g	SODIUM	380 mg

Years ago, one of the best appetizers in my restaurant was the quesadilla. Back then, the service staff had to explain to most guests what a quesadilla was. Today it is as common as the pizza. These turkey quesadillas are low fat, with a hearty taste.

TURKEY QUESADILLAS

Makes 4 servings
Temperature: medium grill or 350°F oven

2 flour tortillas
4 ounces smoked turkey, cut into strips
2 ounces reduced fat Monterey Jack or cheddar, shredded
2 tablespoons salsa

Preheat oven or grill. Lay out two tortillas. Place half the turkey on one side of each tortilla. Place the cheese and salsa on top and fold in half.

Bake or grill for 5 to 8 minutes. Remove; cut into wedges.

NUTRITIONAL INFORMATION

CALORIES 300

PROTEIN	23 g	CHOLESTEROL	29 mg
FAT	10 g	FIBER	2 g
SAT. FAT	4 g	SODIUM	920 mg

This version of a nonfat, high-protein omelette is wonderful to eat after an energy-burning workout. It will replace the vital protein needed to recover from a workout.

OMELETTE

Makes 1 serving

3 egg whites, slightly beaten
1 teaspoon chopped fresh herbs: parsley, basil, cilantro, thyme, or sage
2 drops Tabasco
fresh ground black pepper
vegetable spray

Spray a nonstick omelette, egg, or small sauté pan with vegetable spray and preheat. When the pan becomes hot, pour in the egg whites and allow the eggs to slightly set until the edges begin to bubble. Gather the egg whites toward the center, tilting the pan to allow the uncooked portion to run into the open part of the pan.

Place the herbs, Tabasco, pepper, and filling(s) into the center and, with a spatula, fold the omelette in half and slide onto a plate.

To make a fluffier omelette, whip the egg whites a bit longer and cover the pan while the omelette cooks.

FILLINGS:

fat free cheeses	salsa
grilled chopped chicken	grilled portobella mushrooms
poached salmon	sliced sautéed button or shiitake mushrooms
steamed chopped broccoli	steamed spinach
grilled peppers	marinated tomatoes

NUTRITIONAL INFORMATION
(PLAIN OMELETTE)

CALORIES 50

PROTEIN	12 g	CHOLESTEROL	1 mg
FAT	0 g	FIBER	0 g
SAT. FAT	0 g	SODIUM	160 mg

Breakfast is the most important meal of the day. There's no excuse for missing breakfast when Eggs on the Run are only minutes away!

EGGS ON THE RUN

Makes 1 serving
Temperature: microwave on high

2 ounces egg substitute ($^1/_4$ cup)
1 teaspoon fat free milk
1 tablespoon reduced fat cheese
2 drops Tabasco
fresh ground black pepper
1 8-inch flour tortilla, warmed
vegetable spray

Spray a small microwavable dish with vegetable spray.

Whip the egg with the milk, cheese, Tabasco, and pepper and place in a microwavable dish. Microwave on high for one minute (time is approximate due to various microwaves).

Place a flour tortilla between two paper towels and microwave on high for 30 seconds, or until hot. Remove and roll up the cooked egg mixture in the tortilla before running.

NUTRITIONAL INFORMATION

CALORIES 200

PROTEIN	14 g	CHOLESTEROL	26 mg
FAT	5 g	FIBER	0 g
SAT. FAT	1 g	SODIUM	490 mg

There's nothing better in the morning than a good Southern-style biscuit drizzled with honey. Keep up the tradition by baking this whole wheat version.

WHOLE WHEAT BISCUITS

Makes 12 biscuits
Temperature: 400°F oven

2 cups whole wheat flour
1 cup flour
$^1/_2$ cup margarine
1 cup fat free milk
1 tablespoon white vinegar or lemon juice
1 teaspoon baking powder
pinch salt
$^1/_2$ cup crushed ice
vegetable spray

Preheat oven. Grease a cookie sheet with vegetable spray.

Mix the vinegar or lemon juice with the milk and allow to sit for 10 minutes. Combine the baking powder, salt, whole wheat, and regular flour. Break up the margarine into peanut-size pieces. Add the milk and ice and mix into the flour until it forms a dough.

Lightly flour a wooden board and place the dough on top. Dust lightly with extra flour if the dough is too sticky. Roll out to $^3/_4$ inch thickness and cut into 12 biscuits. Reroll the extra dough without mixing too much (biscuits will become chewy), and cut any extra biscuits.

Place biscuits on a greased cookie sheet. Bake for 10 to 12 minutes.

NUTRITIONAL INFORMATION

CALORIES 170

PROTEIN	5 g	CHOLESTEROL	24 mg
FAT	7 g	FIBER	3 g
SAT. FAT	1.5 g	SODIUM	180 mg

Dumplings are a great way to start any meal. The seasonings can be changed to compliment any flavor. Unlike some that are filled with a blend of meats that make them higher in fat, this version is a winner.

STEAMED BEAN DUMPLINGS

Makes 6 servings

1 cup black beans, canned or cooked and pureed
$^1/_4$ cup Carmelized Onion (see page 105)
6 cloves Carmelized Garlic (see page 104)
1 tablespoon fresh ginger, chopped
1 green onion, chopped
1 teaspoon sesame oil
2 teaspoons lite soy sauce
$^1/_4$ cup unsalted peanuts, chopped
1 12-ounce package wonton wrappers
2 egg whites, slightly beaten

Combine the beans, onion, garlic, ginger, green onion, sesame oil, soy sauce, peanuts, and egg whites.

Place several wonton skins end to end. Wet one corner with a little water. Place one teaspoon of filling in each. Fold the top corner over the filling, making a triangle. Press down and moisten opposite corners. Overlap the opposite ends, forming a little hat, and firmly seal. Repeat until all the filling is used.

Place the wontons in a steamer and steam for 8 to 10 minutes. Serve with Peanut Dipping Sauce (see page 39).

NUTRITIONAL INFORMATION

CALORIES 260

PROTEIN	11 g	CHOLESTEROL	43 mg
FAT	4.5 g	FIBER	4 g
SAT. FAT	0.5 g	SODIUM	650 mg

Use this dipping sauce for a variety of foods such as cut raw vegetables, hard fruits like apples, or pears, seafood, pork, chicken, and dumplings.

PEANUT DIPPING SAUCE

Makes about 1¹/₄ cups

¹/₄ cup lite chunky peanut butter
³/₄ cup apple juice, warmed
3 cloves Carmelized Garlic (see page 104)
1 teaspoon lite soy sauce
1 teaspoon sesame oil
1 tablespoon sesame seeds, toasted
1 teaspoon fresh ginger, chopped
1 teaspoon Tabasco
1 teaspoon fresh cilantro, chopped

Puree the peanut butter with the apple juice, garlic, soy sauce, seseme oil, seseme seeds, ginger, Tabasco, and cilantro. Serve immediately.

NUTRITIONAL INFORMATION
(PER TABLESPOON)

CALORIES 70			
PROTEIN	3 g	CHOLESTEROL	4 mg
FAT	4.5 g	FIBER	1 g
SAT. FAT	1 g	SODIUM	35 mg

Most cornbreads are very high in fat. The flavor does not have to be sacrificed by the reduction of fat in this version.

CHILI CORNBREAD

Makes 1 loaf
Temperature: 400°F oven

6 ounces cornmeal, fine grind maize
5 ounces all-purpose flour
4 teaspoons baking powder
2 tablespoons sugar
1 tablespoon honey
1/2 teaspoon salt
1 cup plain low fat yogurt
2 ounces skim milk
2 egg whites, beaten slightly
4 tablespoons olive oil
2 jalapeño chiles, sliced
4 cloves Caramelized Garlic (see page 104)
1 green onion or scallion, chopped
1/2 red pepper, roasted and chopped
1 tablespoon sesame or poppy seeds, toasted
1 tablespoon fresh cilantro leaves, rough chopped

Preheat the oven. Mix the cornmeal, flour, baking powder, sugar, salt, and honey. Add the yogurt, milk, egg whites, and olive oil. Combine the jalapeños, garlic, green onion or scallion, red pepper, cilantro, and half the sesame seeds, then stir in. Mix all the ingredients until the dough comes together, use caution to not overmix.

Place the cornbread into a greased cake pan. Sprinkle the remaining sesame seeds on top. Bake for 25 to 30 minutes. Cool slightly before removing the bread from the pan.

NUTRITIONAL INFORMATION

CALORIES 170			
PROTEIN	5 g	CHOLESTEROL	0 mg
FAT	6 g	FIBER	2 g
SAT. FAT	1 g	SODIUM	190 mg

SOUPS & STEWS

Summer nights are made for light meals like this stew. The clams will act like a timer. When the shells open, the snapper is done. If fresh clams are not available, cook for 7 to 8 minutes; the snapper will still taste great.

RED SNAPPER AND CLAM STEW

Makes 4 servings

4 6-ounce red snapper fillets
2 dozen littleneck clams, well scrubbed
1 tablespoon olive oil
1 head Caramelized Garlic (see page 104)
2 cups clam juice or vegetable broth
3 tablespoons fresh basil, chopped
1 teaspoon hot red pepper flakes
1/4 cup sliced black olives
freshly ground black pepper

Heat the olive oil in a large casserole or sauté pan.

Add the snapper, clams, garlic, clam juice or vegetable broth, fresh basil, hot red pepper flakes, olives, and freshly ground back pepper. Cover and place on medium heat until the liquid begins to boil. Lower to a simmer and cook for about 8 to 10 minutes.

Clams should all be opened and the snapper will be firm.

NUTRITIONAL INFORMATION

CALORIES 320

PROTEIN	42 g	CHOLESTEROL	17 mg
FAT	8 g	FIBER	1 g
SAT. FAT	1.5 g	SODIUM	700 mg

This tasty meatless chili has plenty of protein and fiber. I like to serve it as a side dish or a hot luncheon choice. The beans provide a steady supply of energy for an active day.

BLACK BEAN CHILI

Makes 6 servings

1 pound uncooked black beans, washed
1 tablespoon olive oil
1 onion, sliced, grilled, and chopped
1 red bell pepper, chopped
1 rib celery, chopped
1 head Caramelized Garlic (see page 104)
2 jalapeño peppers, chopped
2 teaspoons ground cumin
1 teaspoon ground coriander
2 cups tomato sauce
1 cup chicken broth
1 tablespoon balsamic vinegar
1 tablespoon cilantro, coarsely chopped
Tabasco to taste

Preheat a heavy duty soup pot.

Add the olive oil, onion, red bell pepper, celery, garlic, and jalapeños. Cook on medium heat for 2 minutes. Add the cumin and coriander and cook for 1 minute. Add the tomato sauce, chicken broth, balsamic vinegar, black beans, and cilantro.

Bring to a boil and simmer for 1 1/2 to 2 hours, until the beans are tender.

NUTRITIONAL INFORMATION

CALORIES 310

PROTEIN	19 g	CHOLESTEROL	55 mg
FAT	3.5 g	FIBER	18 g
SAT. FAT	0.5 g	SODIUM	530 mg

Vegetable soup has always been one of my favorites during the first autumn days, especially after the garden has provided me with all the delicious ingredients.

VEGETABLE SOUP

Makes 6 servings

2 tablespoons olive oil
1 large onion, chopped
1/2 cup carrots, chopped
1 rib celery, chopped
6 cloves Caramelized Garlic (see page 104)
2 cups cabbage, chopped
1 cup potatoes, chopped
1 15-ounce can corn, with juice
2 cups (or 15 ounces) canned whole tomatoes
2 cups chicken or vegetable broth
1 tablespoon fresh chopped parsley, basil, or cilantro or a combination of each
1 teaspoon Tabasco
fresh ground black pepper

Heat a large soup pot to a medium temperature. Add the olive oil and onion and cook until a light golden color, stirring occasionally. Add the carrots, celery, and garlic and cook for 2 minutes. Add the cabbage; cook for 5 minutes. Add the potatoes, corn, canned tomatoes, chicken or vegetable broth, fresh herbs, Tabasco, and fresh ground black pepper. Bring the soup to a boil, then simmer the soup, uncovered, for 30 minutes.

Optional
Add 1-10 inch shredded flour tortilla for 4 southwest style tortilla soup

NUTRITIONAL INFORMATION

CALORIES 160

PROTEIN	5 g	CHOLESTEROL	25 mg
FAT	6 g	FIBER	4 g
SAT. FAT	1 g	SODIUM	550 mg

There are a lot of ingredients in this recipe; however, it can be prepared very quickly.

CLAM CHOWDER

Makes 6 servings

2 tablespoons olive oil
2 cans chopped clams with juice or 1 cup fresh chopped clams with juice
1 large onion, chopped
1/2 cup carrots, chopped
1 rib celery, chopped
1 green bell pepper, chopped
6 cloves Caramelized Garlic (see page 104)
2 cups potatoes, chopped
1 15-ounce can corn, with juice
1 cup canned whole tomatoes
1 cup clam juice or chicken broth
1 teaspoon rosemary
1 teaspoon thyme
1 teaspoon oregano
1 teaspoon Tabasco
fresh ground black pepper

Heat a large soup pot to a medium temperature. Add the olive oil and onion and cook until a light golden color, stirring occasionally. Add the carrots, celery, bell pepper, and garlic and cook for 2 minutes. Add the potatoes, corn, canned tomatoes, chopped clams and clam juice, rosemary, thyme, oregano, Tabasco, and fresh ground black pepper. Bring the soup to a boil and then simmer for 25 minutes.

NUTRITIONAL INFORMATION

CALORIES 180			
PROTEIN	8 g	CHOLESTEROL	28 mg
FAT	5 g	FIBER	3 g
SAT. FAT	0.5 g	SODIUM	510 mg

The black beans are an excellent source of complex carbohydrates that give you the energy to last all day. As a bonus, the soup also tastes great!

BLACK BEAN & RICE SOUP

Makes 6 servings

2 tablespoons olive oil
1 large onion, chopped
1 red bell pepper, chopped
1 rib celery, chopped
2 green onions, chopped
6 cloves Caramelized Garlic (see page 104)
2 teaspoons cumin
2 cups uncooked black beans, washed
1/2 cup cooked brown rice
8 cups reduced sodium chicken or vegetable broth
1 tablespoon fresh cilantro
1 teaspoon Tabasco
fresh ground black pepper

Heat a large soup pot to a medium temperature. Add the onion and oilive oil, and cook until a light golden color, stirring occasionally. Add the bell pepper, celery, green onions, garlic, and cumin. Cook for 4 to 5 minutes. Add the black beans, chicken or vegetable broth, cilantro, Tabasco, and fresh ground black pepper. Bring the soup to a boil and then simmer for 45 minutes, or until the beans are tender. Mix in cooked rice and serve.

Simmer soup for 30 minutes.

NUTRITIONAL INFORMATION

CALORIES 305

PROTEIN	20 g	CHOLESTEROL	44 mg
FAT	6 g	FIBER	15 g
SAT. FAT	1 g	SODIUM	750 mg

I find that using very simple ingredients makes for great recipes. The proof is in the pot!

ONION & POTATO SOUP

Makes 6 servings

2 tablespoons olive oil
2 large onions, chopped
$^1/_2$ cup leeks, chopped
1 rib celery, chopped
6 cloves Caramelized Garlic (see page 104)
3 cups diced potatoes
6 cups reduced sodium chicken or vegetable broth
1 tablespoon fresh chopped parsley
$^1/_4$ teaspoon nutmeg
1 teaspoon Tabasco
fresh ground black pepper

Heat a large soup pot to a medium temperature. Add the olive oil and onions and cook until a light golden color, stirring occasionally. Add the leeks, celery, and garlic and cook for 2 minutes. Add the potatoes, chicken or vegetable broth, parsley, Tabasco, nutmeg, and fresh ground black pepper. Bring the soup to a boil and then simmer for 25 minutes. Puree one third of the soup in a food mill or blender, return to the soup pot, bring to a boil, and serve.

NUTRITIONAL INFORMATION

CALORIES 130

PROTEIN	5 g	CHOLESTEROL	19 mg
FAT	4.5 g	FIBER	2 g
SAT. FAT	0.5 g	SODIUM	570 mg

I like to take a typical recipe and put a spin on it. Try road testing a few for yourself. That is what cooking is all about.

MINESTRONE WITH SHRIMP VEGETABLE SOUP

Makes 6 servings

2 tablespoons olive oil
1 pound medium shrimp, peeled and deveined
1 large onion, chopped
1/2 cup carrots, chopped
1 rib celery, chopped
1 green bell pepper, chopped
6 cloves Caramelized Garlic (see page 104)
1 cup potatoes, chopped
1 cup white beans, cooked or canned and drained
2 cups canned whole tomatoes
2 cups reduced sodium chicken or vegetable broth
1 cup cooked orzo or other small pasta
1 tablespoon fresh chopped parsley or basil, or a combination of each
1 teaspoon Tabasco
fresh ground black pepper

Heat a large soup pot to a medium temperature. Add the olive oil and onion and cook until a light golden color, stirring occasionally. Add the carrots, celery, green bell pepper, and garlic; cook for 2 minutes. Add the potatoes, canned tomatoes, chicken or vegetable broth, fresh herbs, Tabasco, and fresh ground black pepper. Bring the soup to a boil and simmer for 20 minutes, or until the potatoes are tender. Add the shrimp, cooked beans, and cooked orzo or pasta. Simmer for 5 additional minutes, or until the shrimp is cooked.

NUTRITIONAL INFORMATION

CALORIES 220

PROTEIN	16 g	CHOLESTEROL	28 mg
FAT	6 g	FIBER	3 g
SAT. FAT	1 g	SODIUM	390 mg

True Cajuns may not think that this gumbo is authentic. However, the basic ingredients have been used, with a small fraction of the fat. We can all feel good about that.

TURKEY GUMBO

makes 6 servings

2 tablespoons olive oil
12-ounce turkey tenderloin, diced (may be grilled first for flavor)
$^1/_2$ pound reduced fat smoked turkey sausage, chopped
1 large onion, chopped
1 green bell pepper, chopped
3 green onions, chopped
1 rib celery, chopped
1 cup okra, fresh or frozen, sliced
6 cloves Caramelized Garlic (see page 104)
2 cups (or 15 ounces) canned whole tomatoes
4 cups reduced sodium chicken or vegetable broth
1 tablespoon fresh chopped parsley
1 teaspoon Tabasco
2 teaspoons gumbo file powder dissolved in $^1/_4$ cup chicken broth
fresh ground black pepper

Heat a large soup pot to a medium temperature. Add the olive oil and turkey tenderloin, and turkey sausage. Add the onion and cook until a light golden color, stirring occasionally. Add the green bell pepper, green onions, celery, and garlic and cook for 2 minutes. Add the canned tomatoes, chicken or vegetable broth, parsley, Tabasco, and fresh ground black pepper. Bring the soup to a boil and then simmer for 30 minutes. Add the okra and gumbo file. Simmer the gumbo uncovered for 35 to 45 minutes.

NOTE: Gumbo file powder can be found in the spice section of your market.

NUTRITIONAL INFORMATION

CALORIES 220

PROTEIN	24 g	CHOLESTEROL	11 mg
FAT	9 g	FIBER	2 g
SAT. FAT	2 g	SODIUM	790 mg

Turkey was once served only on special occasions. Today, however, we can give thanks throughout the year because turkeys are always available at a good price—and they're low in fat. Here's a recipe for your leftover turkey.

TURKEY BRUNSWICK STEW

Makes 6 servings

¹/2 cup smoked turkey sausage or kielbasa, chopped
3 cups cooked turkey (remove the skin, debone, and chop)
1 tablespoon olive oil
1 cup onions, chopped
8 cloves Caramelized Garlic (see page 104)
1 teaspoon thyme
1 teaspoon rosemary
2 cups potatoes, washed and chopped
1 16-ounce can corn, with juice
1 28-ounce can plum tomatoes
1 15-ounce can cannellini beans, drained and rinsed
1 teaspoon Tabasco
¹/4 teaspoon nutmeg
fresh ground black pepper

Preheat a large soup or stockpot.

Add the olive oil, turkey sausage or kielbasa, onion, and garlic and lightly brown. Place the cooked turkey in the pot and cook for 3 to 4 minutes. Add the thyme, rosemary, potatoes, corn, tomatoes, beans, Tabasco, and nutmeg. Cover the pot and simmer for 1¹/2 hours, covered.

Add fresh ground black pepper to taste.

NUTRITIONAL INFORMATION

CALORIES 340

PROTEIN	30 g	CHOLESTEROL	39 mg
FAT	8 g	FIBER	6 g
SAT. FAT	2 g	SODIUM	650 mg

This recipe is a nice way to start a heavy meal or can be enjoyed as is, in a minutes!

SOUP IN A MINUTE

Makes 1 serving

12-ounce can reduced sodium, low fat chicken broth
¹/₄ cup snow peas, cut into angled strips
¹/₄ cup spinach leaves, washed well and slightly chopped
2 tablespoons cooked orzo or brown rice
1 teaspooon fresh basil, chopped
pinch nutmeg
fresh ground black pepper

Place the chicken broth and snow peas in a small pot. Bring to a boil. Add the spinach leaves. Lower to a simmer. Add the cooked orzo or rice, basil, nutmeg, and black pepper. Simmer for one minute, uncovered.

NUTRITIONAL INFORMATION

CALORIES 60			
PROTEIN	6 g	CHOLESTEROL	9 mg
FAT	0 g	FIBER	1 g
SAT. FAT	0 g	SODIUM	730 mg

Most pea soups I have prepared are vegetable based or made with the traditional ham bone. With so much turkey prepared today, I use turkey bones as a substitute.

TURKEY PEA SOUP

Makes 6 to 8 servings

2 cups split peas, rinsed in cold water
1/2 cup chopped low fat smoked turkey sausage
1/2 cup onions, chopped
1/4 cup celery, chopped
1/4 cup carrots, chopped
8 cups reduced sodium chicken broth
1/2 cup potatoes, peeled and diced
2 cups cooked lean turkey meat
turkey bones, roasted until brown
2 bay leaves
1 teaspoon Tabasco
fresh ground black pepper

Soak the split peas in a large bowl, covered with cold water, for 8 hours. Drain the peas and discard the water.

Roast the turkey bones until light brown. Preheat a large soup pot. Add the smoked turkey sausage, onions, celery, and carrot. Cook for 5 minutes or until the vegetables are lightly brown.

Add the broth, potatoes, split peas, turkey meat, turkey bones, bay leaves, Tabasco, and black pepper. Bring to a boil, then simmer for 1 hour or until the peas are tender. Remove the turkey bones and discard.

If you like a creamy soup, puree half of the soup in a food processor or blender. Return to the soup pot, bring to a boil to blend, then serve.

NUTRITIONAL INFORMATION

CALORIES 70

PROTEIN	3 g	CHOLESTEROL	4 mg
FAT	4.5 g	FIBER	1 g
SAT. FAT	1 g	SODIUM	35 mg

SALADS

Tired of spinach salads? Add a pair of chopsticks, and you have an ideal hot refreshing dish.

BOK CHOY SALAD

Makes 6 servings
Temperature: grill, wok, or sauté on medium heat

1 head bok choy, with stems, shredded
2 teaspoons sesame oil
1/2 fresh pineapple, cut into chunks
2 scallions
6 cloves Caramelized Garlic (see page 104)
1 tablespoon fresh ginger, peeled and chopped
1 large cucumber, peeled, seeded, and sliced
1 tablespoon honey
3/4 cup bok choy dressing (see page 76)

Preheat a wok or sauté pan. Add the sesame oil, bok choy stems, ginger, garlic, and scallions. Cook for a minute on high. Add the fresh pineapple chunks and honey; cook for 2 minutes. Remove from the heat and cool. Toss with cucumber and shredded greens from the bok choy.

Add bok choy dressing to the salad and marinate for one hour before serving.

NUTRITIONAL INFORMATION

CALORIES 100

PROTEIN	3 g	CHOLESTEROL	18 mg
FAT	3.5 g	FIBER	3 g
SAT. FAT	0 g	SODIUM	40 mg

Have you ever had a chewy, dry steak? Try cooling the steak for about 2 minutes before slicing. This will allow you to slice the meat thinner, ensuring you have very tender pieces to chew.

STEAK ONION SALAD

Makes 4 servings
Temperature: grill high, then medium

2 8- to 10-ounce strip steaks
1 medium red onion, sliced and grilled
6 plum tomatoes, split, seeded, and grilled
3 cups salad greens
$^1/_4$ cup Vinaigrette Dressing (see page 76)
freshly ground black pepper
$^1/_2$ cup croutons

Preheat the grill.

Grill the steaks on high for 2 minutes on each side, then put at a medium temperature for 4 to 5 minutes, or until desired doneness. Remove and let cool.

Slice the steaks thinly. In a medium bowl combine the sliced steak, grilled red onion, tomatoes, and vinaigrette. Place over salad greens. Top with croutons and black pepper.

NUTRITIONAL INFORMATION

CALORIES 230

PROTEIN	26 g	CHOLESTEROL	9 mg
FAT	9 g	FIBER	4 g
SAT. FAT	3.5 g	SODIUM	130 mg

Just like spinach, arugula can contain a lot of sand in the leaves. To prepare, first remove any brown from the stem ends. Then soak in a large pot of cold water, lift out the leaves, and keep replacing the water until it is dirt-free.

ARUGULA WALNUT SALAD

Makes 4 servings

6 cups arugula, washed and dried
1 head radicchio, chopped
1/4 cup walnuts, toasted
1 apple, sliced and grilled
2 tablespoons shaved Parmigiano-Reggiano cheese
2 tablespoons olive oil
juice from 2 lemons

Toss together the arugula, radicchio, walnuts, apple, and cheese. Drizzle the olive oil and lemon juice on top.

NUTRITIONAL INFORMATION

CALORIES 150

PROTEIN	4 g	CHOLESTEROL	10 mg
FAT	11 g	FIBER	2 g
SAT. FAT	2 g	SODIUM	70 mg

Making a large turkey will leave plenty for leftovers and this salad recipe.

TURKEY AND PECAN SALAD

Makes 4 servings
Temperature: grill medium, then low

2 10 ounce fresh turkey tenderloins
1 cup Grilling Marinade (see page 160)
$^1/_2$ cup toasted pecans
$^1/_2$ cup sliced strawberries
3 cups mixed salad greens, washed & dried (e.g., romaine, radicchio, endive)
$^1/_4$ cup blue cheese or Gorgonzola, crumbled
$^1/_4$ cup Fruit Dressing (see page 83)

Marinate the turkey tenderloins in the grilling marinade in a refrigerated bowl for 2 hours or overnight.

Preheat the grill. Remove the turkey from the marinade and grill on medium heat for 3 to 4 minutes on each side. When the tenderloin is slightly brown, reduce the heat to low and continue cooking for an additional 5 to 6 minutes, to an internal temperature of 160°F. Remove and cool. Slice the tenderloins. Combine the salad greens, strawberries, pecans, and cheese. Add the sliced turkey tenderloins and serve with fruit dressing.

NUTRITIONAL INFORMATION

CALORIES 260

PROTEIN	33 g	CHOLESTEROL	7 mg
FAT	11 g	FIBER	2 g
SAT. FAT	2 g	SODIUM	180 mg

Food and eating are a celebration. That's why I like to enhance basic recipes. Eating fresh tuna will make it difficult to go back to canned. Although I eat a lot of tuna from the can, sometimes I have to one-up it!

AHI TUNA SALAD

Makes 4 servings
Temperature: grill high, then low

1¹/2 pounds tuna steak
¹/2 cup Fish Marinade (see page 161)
2 tablespoons lowfat plain yogurt
2 tablespoons low fat mayonnaise
2 tablespoons onion, chopped fine
¹/2 lemon, juice only, per serving of fish
2 cloves Caramelized Garlic (see page 104)
1 tablespoon sweet pickle relish per serving of fish
2 plum tomatoes, seeded and chopped

Marinate tuna for an hour in the refrigerator. Preheat the grill. Grill the tuna on high for 2 to 3 minutes on each side. Lower the heat and cook until tuna reaches the desired doneness.

Remove the tuna and allow to cool slightly. Slice, then toss with yogurt, mayonnaise, onion, lemon, garlic, relish, and tomatoes.

Serve open-faced on toasted bread or with salad greens.

NUTRITIONAL INFORMATION

CALORIES 300

PROTEIN	39 g	CHOLESTEROL	23 mg
FAT	6 g	FIBER	1 g
SAT. FAT	1.5 g	SODIUM	470 mg

Adding tomatoes to the potato salad will keep it moist and add color. Always keep any salad in the refrigerator or chilled at 40°F if not a vinaigrette dressing

POTATO AND TOMATO
SALAD

≈≈≈≈≈≈

Makes 4 servings

1 pound potatoes (red, Yukon, or all-purpose)
2 cups plum tomatoes, seeded and chopped
2 scallions, chopped
2 tablespoons prepared mustard
4 tablespoons red wine vinegar
2 tablespoons olive oil
6 cloves Caramelized Garlic (see page 104)
2 tablespoons fresh basil, chopped
freshly ground black pepper

Cook the potatoes in lightly salted water until just tender, 18 to 20 minutes. Cool.

Cut the potatoes into 1-inch pieces. In a medium bowl combine the scallions, mustard, vinegar, olive oil, garlic, basil, and black pepper.

Toss with the tomatoes and marinate for 30 minutes before serving.

NUTRITIONAL INFORMATION

CALORIES 170			
PROTEIN	3 g	CHOLESTEROL	27 mg
FAT	7 g	FIBER	3 g
SAT. FAT	1 g	SODIUM	110 mg

Throughout my years of cooking experience, I have noticed that shrimp is rarely passed up when it is offered. Here is yet another reason to enjoy it!

SHRIMP SALAD

Makes 4 servings

20 medium cooked shrimp (about 1 pound), peeled, devined, grilled or boiled
1 cup red new potatoes, cooked and chopped small
1/4 cup Caramelized Onion (see page 105)
1/2 cup plain lowfat yogurt
2 tablespoons mustard
1 tablespoon ketchup
1 lemon, juice only
1 tablespoon chives or 1 green onion, chopped
1/4 cup pineapple, apple, or pear, chopped
1/2 teaspoon fresh thyme
1 teaspoon Tabasco
fresh ground pepper

Mix the onion, yogurt, mustard, ketchup, lemon juice, chives or onion, fruit, thyme, Tabasco, and fresh ground black pepper. Add the potatoes and cooked shrimp. Refrigerate for an hour before serving.

Serve over mixed greens or in a flour tortilla sandwich wrap.

NUTRITIONAL INFORMATION

CALORIES 120			
PROTEIN	17 g	CHOLESTEROL	8 mg
FAT	1.5 g	FIBER	0 g
SAT. FAT	0 g	SODIUM	135 mg

I maintain healthy eating habits because I actually enjoy eating this way. Part of having an enjoyable lifestyle means eating quality meats and seafood. When fresh tuna is available, I will prepare a variety of dishes, including a spin-off of the traditional canned version.

TUNA SALAD

Makes 2 servings

1 10-ounce can solid white albacore tuna packed in water, or cooked tuna steak
2 tablespoons reduced fat mayonnaise
1 teaspoon mustard
1 tablespoon sweet pickle relish
1 tablespoon chives or 1 green onion, chopped
$^1/_2$ lemon, juice only
$^1/_2$ teaspoon Tabasco
fresh ground black pepper
2 hard boiled egg whites, chopped (optional)

Flake the tuna in a bowl. Add the mayonnaise, mustard, relish, chives, lemon juice, Tabasco, black pepper, and hard-boiled egg whites. Mix well and refrigerate for an hour.

ADDITIONAL VARIATIONS:

grapes
apple slices
chopped tomatoes

pineapple chunks
chopped walnuts

NUTRITIONAL INFORMATION

CALORIES 200

PROTEIN	27 g	CHOLESTEROL	4 mg
FAT	8 g	FIBER	0 g
SAT. FAT	1.5 g	SODIUM	530 mg

I have never been a fan of mayonnaise. There are many tastier, healthier alternatives. This Pacific or Asian-style tuna salad without the mayo is the real magilla!

PACIFIC TUNA SALAD

Makes 2 servings

1 10-ounce tuna steak, cooked
1 tablespoon olive oil
3 cloves Caramelized Garlic (see page 104)
1 teaspoon mustard
1 teaspoon ginger
1 teaspoon light or low sodium soy sauce
1/2 teaspoon sesame oil
2 teaspoons sesame seeds, toasted
1 tablespoon honey
1 tablespoon cilantro, chopped
1 tablespoon chives or 1 green onion, chopped
1/2 lemon, juice only
1/2 teaspoon Tabasco
fresh ground black pepper

Flake the tuna in a bowl. Add the olive oil, garlic, mustard, ginger, soy sauce, sesame oil, sesame seeds, honey, cilantro, chives or onion, lemon juice, Tabasco, and black pepper. Mix well and refrigerate for an hour.

NUTRITIONAL INFORMATION

CALORIES 360

PROTEIN	39 g	CHOLESTEROL	11 mg
FAT	17 g	FIBER	0 g
SAT. FAT	3.5 g	SODIUM	240 mg

This hearty luncheon salad will get you through a busy afternoon.

TUNA CHEF SALAD

Makes 2 servings

Pacfic Tuna Salad (see page 62)
2 cups mixed salad greens
2 tomatoes, quartered
2 green onions, chopped
1/4 cup white beans, cooked or canned
1/4 cup mushrooms, sliced
2 tablespoons fat free chow mein noodles

Arrange the tuna salad on a bed of the mixed greens. Place the tomatoes, green onions, white beans, and mushrooms around plate. Top with chow mein noodles and serve.

NUTRITIONAL INFORMATION

CALORIES 440

PROTEIN	43 g	CHOLESTEROL	29 mg
FAT	18 g	FIBER	4 g
SAT. FAT	3.5 g	SODIUM	420 mg

This is a great make-ahead salad. Mix all the ingredients in advance, but leave out the salad greens and feta cheese until just before serving.

CHOPPED GREEK SALAD

Makes 4 servings

3 cups mixed salad greens
2 tomatoes, chopped
1 cucumber, peeled and chopped
2 green onions, chopped
1 cup chopped pickled mixed vegetables—carrots, broccoli, cauliflower, peppers, and mushrooms
1/4 cup cured black olives
1/4 cup feta cheese, crumbled
1/4 cup cooked chickpeas, drained
1/4 cup Italian Dressing (see page 78)
1 teaspoon rosemary
1/4 teaspoon thyme

Mix the salad greens, tomatoes, cucumber, green onions, mixed pickled vegetables, olives, feta cheese, and chickpeas. Add the rosemary and thyme to the dressing; pour over the salad. Toss, then top with feta cheese.

NUTRITIONAL INFORMATION

CALORIES 110			
PROTEIN	5 g	CHOLESTEROL	14 mg
FAT	5 g	FIBER	4 g
SAT. FAT	2 g	SODIUM	550 mg

The citrus flavor of the orange is a great complement to the beets. It took me many years to acquire a taste for beets. Here is the first version I took a liking to.

SPINACH SALAD AND BEETS

Makes 2 servings

3 cups spinach, cleaned
$^1/_4$ cup sliced mushrooms
$^1/_2$ cup pickled sliced beets
3 cloves Caramelized Garlic (see page 104)
$^1/_4$ cup sliced red onion
1 orange, peeled and segmented
$^1/_4$ cup orange juice
2 tablespoons balsamic vinegar
1 teaspoon Tabasco
1 tablespoon honey
pinch nutmeg
pinch allspice
fresh ground black pepper

Mix the beets, garlic, red onion, orange segments, orange juice, balsamic vinegar, Tabasco, honey, nutmeg, allspice and fresh ground black pepper. Marinate for one hour.

Arrange the spinach and mushrooms on plates. Top with beets and marinade.

NUTRITIONAL INFORMATION

CALORIES 130			
PROTEIN	4 g	CHOLESTEROL	0 mg
FAT	0 g	FIBER	4 g
SAT. FAT	0 g	SODIUM	170 mg

Almost all meats and seafood are great ingredients for a Caesar salad. Shrimp is one especially tasty choice.

SHRIMP OR CHICKEN CAESAR SALAD

Makes 2 servings

3 cups romaine lettuce, chopped
$^1/_2$ pound (14 medium) shrimp (peeled deveined and cooked), or 8-ounce cooked chicken breast
$^1/_4$ cup roasted, grilled, or pickled peppers, chopped
$^1/_4$ cup black olives, sliced
2 tablespoons fat free parmesan cheese
$^1/_4$ cup toasted and chopped French bread croutons
4 tablespoons Caesar Salad Dressing (see page 77)

Mix the lettuce, shrimp or chicken, peppers, olives, parmesan cheese, croutons, and dressing.

Serve on chilled plates.

NUTRITIONAL INFORMATION

CALORIES 190

PROTEIN	23 g	CHOLESTEROL	15 mg
FAT	5 g	FIBER	2 g
SAT. FAT	1.5 g	SODIUM	570 mg

There is nothing like walking out to the garden and picking vine-ripened tomatoes. Today, you can even get tomatoes on the vine at most markets.

SOUTHWEST TOMATO SALAD

Makes 4 servings

2 cups salad greens
6 vine-ripened tomatoes, cut into wedges
$^1/_4$ cup black olives, sliced
$^1/_4$ cup green olives, sliced
2 jalepeños, sliced
2 green onions, chopped
1 red onion, sliced
$^1/_4$ cup cooked red beans
$^1/_4$ cup Italian Dressing (see page 78)
1 tablespoon cilantro, chopped
$^1/_2$ teaspon cumin
10 baked corn tortilla chips, roughly crushed

Mix the dressing, cilantro, and cumin and add to the tomatoes, black olives, green olives, jalepeños, green onions, red beans, and red onion. Marinate for one hour.

Serve over salad greens and top with crushed corn tortilla chips.

NUTRITIONAL INFORMATION

CALORIES 130

PROTEIN	4 g	CHOLESTEROL	20 mg
FAT	4.5 g	FIBER	5 g
SAT. FAT	0.5 g	SODIUM	250 mg

Served cold or warm, this is a very satisfying salad.

PEPPERED STEAK SALAD

Makes 6 servings
Temperature: grill high, then medium

2 pounds flank steak
3 red, yellow, or green peppers—split, seeded, and cut into finger-size pieces
4 tablespoons lite soy sauce
2 tablespoons cider vinegar
1 head Carmelized Garlic (see page 104)
1 tablespoon fresh ginger, chopped
2 teaspoons sesame oil
2 tablespoons honey
9 cups salad greens

Marinate the steak with the soy sauce, vinegar, garlic, ginger, sesame oil, and honey. Refrigerate for 2 hours.

Preheat grill to high. Cook the steak for 4 to 5 minutes and turn; cook until desired doneness. Allow meat to rest for about 5 minutes before slicing into and then across the grain. Grill the peppers and toss in a pan with sliced steak. Serve over mixed greens.

NUTRITIONAL INFORMATION

CALORIES 130

PROTEIN	35 g	CHOLESTEROL	14 mg
FAT	12 g	FIBER	3 g
SAT. FAT	5 g	SODIUM	80 mg

Mesclun is a mixture of several baby greens that lend themselves to being served with foods delicate in flavor and texture. Keep the greens chilled until just before serving to keep them from wilting.

MESCLUN SALAD WITH AHI TUNA

Makes 4 servings
Temperature: grill or cook on high

4 cups mesclun
1 1/2 pounds ahi tuna, sliced two inches thick
2 tablespoons prepared mustard
2 tablespoons crushed black peppercorns
1 tablespoon cilantro, chopped
juice of 2 limes
1/4 cup cured black olives, pitted
1/2 cup red bell pepper, grilled and chopped

Preheat grill or a nonstick sauté pan. Coat the tuna with mustard. Mix the peppercorns and cilantro and cover the tuna.

Sear the tuna on a very hot grill or in a sauté pan and cook 2 minutes on each side. Remove and slice very thinly. Place while still hot on the mesclun greens. Top with the fresh lime juice, olives, and red pepper. Serve immediately.

NUTRITIONAL INFORMATION

CALORIES 280			
PROTEIN	41 g	CHOLESTEROL	7 mg
FAT	10 g	FIBER	2 g
SAT. FAT	2.5 g	SODIUM	240 mg

Today the world's food basket is as close as a trip to your local market. Celebrate the flavors of the tropics with this simple fruit salad. The key is in the ripeness of the fruit!

PAPAYA AND MANGO SALAD

Serves 4

2 medium ripe papayas, peeled and seeded
2 ripe mangos, peeled and pitted
2 cups watercress or bitter greens such as arugula or chicory
1 tablespoon cilantro
juice of 2 limes
4 strawberries, sliced for garnish

Cut the papaya and mango into 1-inch slices. Top with the lime juice and cilantro. Cover and marinate for 30 minutes. Do not refrigerate.

   Place the watercress or bitter greens on four plates. Top with papaya and mango. Garnish with sliced strawberries.

NUTRITIONAL INFORMATION

CALORIES 160			
PROTEIN	2 g	CHOLESTEROL	40 mg
FAT	0.5 g	FIBER	6 g
SAT. FAT	0 g	SODIUM	15 mg

This creamy salad is a favorite that I serve with grilled chicken. Don't let anyone know it contains less fat than the standard potato salad!

CREAMY POTATO SALAD WITH TOMATOES

Makes 4 servings
Temperature: grill medium-low

1 pound red potatoes
2 cups plum tomatoes, grilled, seeded, and chopped
2 scallions, chopped
2 tablespoons prepared mustard
2 tablespoons olive oil
6 cloves Caramelized Garlic (see page 104)
2 tablespoons fresh basil, chopped
fresh ground black pepper
1 cup Yogurt Honey Dressing (see page 75)

Cook the potatoes in lightly salted water until tender, 18 to 20 minutes. Cool. Cut into 1-inch pieces. In a medium bowl combine the scallions, mustard, olive oil, garlic, basil, and black pepper.

Mix the dressing and tomatoes with the potatoes and marinate overnight in the refrigerator, or for at least 30 minutes before serving.

NUTRITIONAL INFORMATION

CALORIES 230			
PROTEIN	5 g	CHOLESTEROL	39 mg
FAT	7 g	FIBER	3 g
SAT. FAT	1 g	SODIUM	140 mg

Vinaigrettes were traditionally used to preserve food. There's nothing wrong with a little tradition. You can marinate meats, seafood, fruits, or vegetables, as in this recipe. The result will be a better dish prepared ahead of time, to avoid a last-minute rush.

BROCCOLI & ORANGE VINAIGRETTE SALAD

2 cups broccoli, parboiled
2 cups orange, peeled and sliced
1 cup mushrooms, parboiled
1 cup cooked red kidney beans
$^{1}/_{2}$ medium red onion, sliced
$^{1}/_{2}$ cup baby carrots
$^{1}/_{2}$ pint cherry tomatoes
$^{1}/_{4}$ cup Vinaigrette Dressing (see page 76)

Combine all the ingredients. Marinate in the refrigerator overnight or for 3 to 4 hours unrefrigerated.

NUTRITIONAL INFORMATION

CALORIES 100

PROTEIN	5 g	CHOLESTEROL	20 mg
FAT	1 g	FIBER	6 g
SAT. FAT	0 g	SODIUM	150 mg

Remove the seeds from the cucumbers to reduce the aftershock in the stomach!

CUCUMBER AND ONION SALAD

≈≈≈≈≈≈≈≈≈≈

Makes 4 servings

2 cucumbers, peeled, halved, and seeded
2 Vidalia onions, or other sweet onions, sliced
6 cloves Caramelized Garlic (see page 104)
1 cup low fat sour cream
3 tablespoons cider vinegar
1 teaspoon dried oregano
1 teaspoon dried thyme
1 teaspoon dry mustard
$^1/_2$ teaspoon hot sauce
fresh ground black pepper

Steam or sauté the onions to slightly soften, then chill.

In a medium bowl combine the garlic, sour cream, vinegar, oregano, thyme, dry mustard, hot sauce, and black pepper; mix well. Thinly slice the cucumbers. Add the cucumbers and chilled onions to the sour cream mixture and mix well.

Marinate in the refrigerator for at least 2 hours before serving.

NUTRITIONAL INFORMATION

CALORIES 130			
PROTEIN	6 g	CHOLESTEROL	15 mg
FAT	5 g	FIBER	2 g
SAT. FAT	4 g	SODIUM	45 mg

DRESSINGS & SAUCES

Honey is an excellent complement to the tartness of the yogurt.

YOGURT HONEY DRESSING

Makes 2 cups

1¹/2 cups plain low fat yogurt
1 fresh lime, juice only
¹/4 cup honey
1 teaspoon Tabasco
1 teaspoon fresh basil
fresh ground black pepper

Mix the yogurt and lime juice. Add honey and stir in Tabasco, basil, and fresh ground black pepper. Refrigerate the dressing for an hour before using.

NUTRITIONAL INFORMATION
(PER 2 TABLESPOONS)

CALORIES 30

PROTEIN	1 g	CHOLESTEROL	6 mg
FAT	0 g	FIBER	0 g
SAT. FAT	0 g	SODIUM	15 mg

A dressing of any type is always best made ahead. Do not refrigerate the vinaigrette if you are using it within the same day.

VINAIGRETTE DRESSING

Makes about 1 cup

¹/2 cup olive oil
¹/4 cup balsamic vinegar
1 tablespoon mustard
4 cloves Caramelized Garlic (see page 104)
1 teaspoon dried basil
1 teaspoon Tabasco
fresh ground black pepper

Combine the oil and vinegar well. Add the mustard, garlic, dried basil, Tabasco, and fresh ground black pepper. Allow the vinaigrette to sit at room temperature for a day to improve its flavor.

VARIATION:

For Bok Choy Dressing, substitute 1 tablespoon fresh cilantro leaves for the basil, and add 1 tablespoon fresh ginger, peeled and chopped.

NUTRITIONAL INFORMATION (PER 2 TABLESPOONS)

CALORIES 30

PROTEIN	0 g	CHOLESTEROL	3 mg
FAT	2 g	FIBER	0 g
SAT. FAT	0 g	SODIUM	105 mg

Hail Caesar! Even the emperor would be satisfied with this very low fat, no anchovy version of the classic.

CAESAR SALAD DRESSING

Makes 1 cup

1/2 cup plain low fat yogurt
1/2 cup fat free sour cream
1 tablespoon lemon juice
4 cloves Caramelized Garlic, crushed (see page 104)
2 tablespoons grated Parmesan cheese
1/2 teaspoon Tabasco
fresh ground black pepper

Mix the yogurt, sour cream, lemon juice, garlic, Parmesan cheese, Tabasco, and fresh ground black pepper. Refrigerate for at least an hour.

NUTRITIONAL INFORMATION
(PER 2 TABLESPOONS)

CALORIES 35

PROTEIN	3 g	CHOLESTEROL	5 mg
FAT	0.5 g	FIBER	0 g
SAT. FAT	0 g	SODIUM	55 mg

Make this dressing in quantity and use it for salads and marinades. Try to make the dressing a day in advance to allow the flavors to bloom.

ITALIAN DRESSING

Makes 1 cup

¹/₄ cup red wine vinegar
2 tablespoons balsamic vinegar
2 tablespoons olive oil
¹/₂ cup tomato or vegetable juice
4 cloves Caramelized Garlic (see page 104)
1 teaspoon basil
1 teaspoon oregano
1 teaspoon paprika
¹/₂ teaspoon dry mustard
1 tablespoon parmesan cheese
¹/₂ teaspoon Tabasco
fresh ground black pepper

Mix the red wine vinegar with the balsamic vinegar and olive oil. Add the tomato juice, garlic, basil, oregano, paprika, dry mustard, parmesan cheese, Tabasco, and fresh ground black pepper.

Allow the dressing to sit at room temperature for an hour before serving.

NUTRITIONAL INFORMATION
(PER 2 TABLESPOONS)

CALORIES 45			
PROTEIN	1 g	CHOLESTEROL	2 mg
FAT	3.5 g	FIBER	0 g
SAT. FAT	0.5 g	SODIUM	65 mg

The secret of this dressing is in the balsamic vinegar. Although aged balsamic vinegar can be more expensive than some wine varieties, there's no need to break the budget—just use a moderately priced brand. You will even be able to find some quality brands packaged under a supermarket label.

BALSAMIC VINEGAR BASIL DRESSING

Makes 1 cup

1/2 cup balsamic vinegar
2 tablespoons olive oil
1/4 cup tomato or vegetable juice
1/4 cup fresh basil, washed, dried, and chopped fine
3 cloves Caramelized Garlic (see page 104)
1/2 teaspoon Tabasco
fresh ground black pepper

Mix the balsamic vinegar, olive oil, tomato or vegetable juice, basil, garlic, Tabasco, and fresh ground black pepper.

Allow the dressing to sit, covered, at room temperature for an hour prior to serving.

NUTRITIONAL INFORMATION
(PER 2 TABLESPOONS)

CALORIES 45			
PROTEIN	0 g	CHOLESTEROL	3 mg
FAT	3.5 g	FIBER	0 g
SAT. FAT	0 g	SODIUM	60 mg

Make this dressing at least 2 hours in advance and refrigerate until ready to use.

RANCH DRESSING

Makes 1 cup

1/2 cup plain low fat yogurt
1/4 fat free sour cream
2 green onions, chopped
1 teaspoon lite or low sodium soy sauce
2 tablespoons ketchup
2 tablespoons mustard
1 tablespoon horseradish
4 cloves Caramelized Garlic (see page 104)
1 teaspoon Tabasco
fresh ground black pepper

Mix the yogurt, sour cream, green onions, soy sauce, ketchup, mustard, horseradish, garlic, Tabasco, and fresh ground black pepper.

Refrigerate for an hour before serving.

NUTRITIONAL INFORMATION
(PER 2 TABLESPOONS)

CALORIES 30

PROTEIN	2 g	CHOLESTEROL	5 mg
FAT	0 g	FIBER	0 g
SAT. FAT	0 g	SODIUM	160 mg

This dressing will taste great not only on salad greens, but also on meats, seafood, or vegetables.

SESAME SEED DRESSING

Makes 1 cup

2 tablespoons sesame seeds, toasted
1/4 cup cider vinegar
1/2 cup apple juice
2 green onions, chopped
4 cloves Caramelized Garlic (see page 104)
1 tablespoon honey
1 teaspoon sesame seed oil
juice of one orange
1 teaspoon Tabasco

Mix all the ingredients well.
　Serve with a spinach salad or mixed greens.

NUTRITIONAL INFORMATION
(PER 2 TABLESPOONS)

CALORIES 40			
PROTEIN	1 g	CHOLESTEROL	7 mg
FAT	1.5 g	FIBER	0 g
SAT. FAT	0 g	SODIUM	0 mg

Toasting the nuts gives a sweeter taste to the dressing. Add fresh strawberries to the salad to complement the fruit in the dressing.

RASPBERRY WALNUT DRESSING

Makes 1 cup

¹/2 cup raspberries or strawberries
¹/4 cup apple juice
2 tablespoons apple cider vinegar
2 tablespoons walnuts, chopped and toasted
1 tablespoon honey
1 tablespoon chives or 1 green onion, chopped

Puree the raspberries or strawberries with the apple juice and apple cider vinegar in a food processor or blender. Pour the mixture through a fine strainer to remove the seeds. Mix in the walnuts, honey, and chives.

Allow to sit for an hour before serving.

NUTRITIONAL INFORMATION (PER 2 TABLESPOONS)

CALORIES 30			
PROTEIN	1 g	CHOLESTEROL	4 mg
FAT	1 g	FIBER	0 g
SAT. FAT	0 g	SODIUM	0 mg

Eating preferences change throughout the seasons. A fruit dressing celebrates the balmy days of summer.

FRUIT DRESSING

Makes 1¹/₄ cups

¹/₂ cup strawberry puree
¹/₂ cup orange juice
1 tablespoon cider vinegar
1 tablespoon balsamic vinegar
1 green onion, chopped
1 tablespoon honey
1 teaspoon Tabasco
fresh ground black pepper

Combine all the ingredients and mix well. Refrigerate for 2 to 3 hours or overnight before serving.

NOTE: Strawberry puree can be made by placing sliced berries and a little lemon or orange juice in a food processor or blender. Blend until pureed, then pass the puree through a fine strainer to remove the seeds.

NUTRITIONAL INFORMATION
(PER 2 TABLESPOONS)

CALORIES 20

PROTEIN	0 g	CHOLESTEROL	5 mg
FAT	0 g	FIBER	0 g
SAT. FAT	0 g	SODIUM	5 mg

Sauces can make or break some dishes. Cocktail shrimp will make a dish with-out the fat. This sauce is also an excellent complement to swordfish.

COCKTAIL SAUCE

Makes about 1 cup

1/2 cup plain low fat yogurt
2 tablespoons ketchup
1 tablespoon dijon mustard
1 tablespoon horseradish
1 tablespoon honey
1 tablespoon fresh lemon juice
3 cloves Carmelized Garlic (see page 104)
1 green onion, chopped
1 teaspoon Tabasco

Mix all the ingredients until combined. Refrigerate for at least an hour before serving.

NUTRITIONAL INFORMATION
(PER 2 TABLESPOONS)

CALORIES 50			
PROTEIN	2 g	CHOLESTEROL	10 mg
FAT	0 g	FIBER	0 g
SAT. FAT	0 g	SODIUM	210 mg

High fat mayonnaise pales in comparison to this zippy nonfat spread. If you would like to make extra, just store it in a tightly covered container in the refrigerator for up to one week.

SANDWICH SPREAD

Makes about 1 cup

$^1/_2$ cup plain low fat yogurt
$^1/_4$ cup fat free sour cream
2 tablespoons dijon mustard
1 tablespoon horseradish
4 cloves Caramelized Garlic (see page 104)
1 green onion, chopped
1 teaspoon Tabasco

Combine all the ingredients well.

NUTRITIONAL INFORMATION
(PER 2 TABLESPOONS)

CALORIES 15			
PROTEIN	1 g	CHOLESTEROL	2 mg
FAT	0 g	FIBER	0 g
SAT. FAT	0 g	SODIUM	60 mg

Cacciatore means "in the style of the hunter."

CACCIATORE SAUCE

Makes about 2 pints

3 cups plum tomatoes, seeded and chopped
1 tablespoon olive oil
1 cup white wine
1 cup chicken or vegetable broth
8 cloves Caramelized Garlic (see page 104)
2 tablespoons fresh basil, rough chopped
fresh ground black pepper

Preheat a saucepan. Add the olive oil, tomatoes, and garlic. Simmer for 2 to 3 minutes. Add the white wine, chicken or vegetable broth, fresh basil, and fresh ground black pepper. Simmer for 10 to 15 minutes and serve.

NUTRITIONAL INFORMATION
(PER ¼ CUP)

CALORIES 60

PROTEIN	1 g	CHOLESTEROL	4 mg
FAT	2 g	FIBER	1 g
SAT. FAT	0 g	SODIUM	80 mg

The vodka gives a certain smoothness to the sauce. Of course the sauce can be made without the vodka, if you choose.

VODKA SAUCE

Makes 2 cups

2 cups tomato sauce
6 plum tomatoes, split and grilled
2 ounces vodka
2 tablespoons fresh basil, chopped
6 cloves Caramelized Garlic (see page 104)
$^1/_2$ teaspoon hot sauce

Preheat a saucepan on the grill or side burner. Add the tomato sauce, tomatoes, vodka, fresh basil, garlic, and hot sauce. Bring to a boil, then lower the temperature, cover, and simmer for 15 minutes.

NUTRITIONAL INFORMATION
(PER ½ CUP)

CALORIES 100			
PROTEIN	3 g	CHOLESTEROL	15 mg
FAT	0.5 g	FIBER	3 g
SAT. FAT	0 g	SODIUM	750 mg

Sharp flavors such as vinegar, garlic, and onion go very well with the sweetness of the mango. Use only a ripe mango, which should smell sweet and feel slightly soft to the touch. Do not refrigerate the mango; it will lose flavor.

MANGO RELISH

makes 4 servings

1 large ripe mango, peeled, deseeded, and rough chopped
2 tbsp balsamic vinegar
1 clove Caramelized Garlic (see page 104)
1/4 cup Caramelized Onion (see page 105)
1 teaspoon Tabasco

Combine all ingedients and allow the flavors of the relish to come together for an hour before serving at room temperature. Do not refrigerate.

NUTRITIONAL INFORMATION
(PER 2 TABLESPOONS)

CALORIES 45			
PROTEIN	1 g	CHOLESTEROL	12 mg
FAT	0 g	FIBER	1 g
SAT. FAT	0 g	SODIUM	0 mg

PASTA & RICE

Once the vodka cooks out of the sauce, it leaves a sweet taste. Just add a salad to complete this meal.

FETTUCINE AND STEAK WITH VODKA SAUCE

Makes 4 servings
Temperature: grill medium, then low

12 ounces fettucine, cooked al dente
1 pound beef flank steak
4 cloves Caramelized Garlic (see page 104)
1 teaspoon dried oregano
1 teaspoon dried thyme
1 teaspoon dried rosemary
1 teaspoon freshly ground black pepper
2 cups Vodka Sauce (see page 87)
grated cheese (optional)

Preheat the grill.

Season the steak with the garlic, oregano, thyme, rosemary, and and fresh ground black pepper. Grill the meat for 4 to 5 minutes on each side.

Remove from the grill and let the meat rest for 5 minutes before slicing across the grain. Slice thin and combine with the cooked fettucine and vodka sauce. You may want to top with grated cheese.

NUTRITIONAL INFORMATION

CALORIES 500

PROTEIN	35 g	CHOLESTEROL	58 mg
FAT	11 g	FIBER	6 g
SAT. FAT	4.5 g	SODIUM	830 mg

Cut down the fat grams by using turkey in place of beef in the chili. You'll feel great about the lower fat grams.

CAVATELLI PASTA WITH
TURKEY CHILI

Makes 6 servings
Temperature: grill high, then low

1 pound cavatelli pasta, cooked
1¹/2 pounds lean ground turkey (chill to form into silver dollar-size burgers)
¹/2 onion, sliced, grilled, and chopped
1 head Caramelized Garlic (see page 104)
1 tablespoon olive oil
3 jalapeños, split, seeded, and chopped
1 tablespoon ground cumin
1 teaspoon dried thyme
1 teaspoon dried rosemary
1 cup tomato sauce
1 cup chili sauce or ketchup
1 tablespoon lite soy sauce
1 tablespoon grated horseradish
2 scallions, chopped
1 cup red beans, canned or cooked
1 tablespoon cilantro
Tabasco to taste

Preheat the grill. Grill the mini turkey burgers over high heat until fully cooked. Remove and cool. Heat a large soup pot. Add the olive oil, onion, garlic, and jalapeños and cook for 5 minutes. Add the cumin, thyme, rosemary, tomato sauce, chili sauce or ketchup, soy sauce, and horseradish; bring to a boil. Lower the temperature, add the turkey burgers, and simmer for 1 hour. Add the scallions and beans and cook for 15 minutes, then add the cilantro and Tabasco.

Add the cooked cavatelli pasta to the turkey chili, mix well, and serve.

NUTRITIONAL INFORMATION

CALORIES 390			
PROTEIN	29 g	CHOLESTEROL	45 mg
FAT	10 g	FIBER	5 g
SAT. FAT	3 g	SODIUM	600 mg

I usually make a large lasagna, then freeze smaller portions. Dinner will be ready after reheating in the microwave.

VEGETABLE LASAGNA

Serves 8

Temperature: grill medium, then low, or bake at 350°F

1 pound lasagna pasta
1 10-ounce package frozen chopped spinach, defrosted and squeezed dry
1 Caramelized Onion, sliced (see page 105)
8 cloves Caramelized Garlic (see page 104)
1 cup sliced mushrooms
3 red bell peppers, split, seeded, and grilled or roasted
1/2 cup artichoke hearts, packed in water
2 10³/4-ounce cans reduced fat cream of mushroom soup
1 cup part-skim shredded mozzarella cheese
4 tablespoons parmesan cheese
1 cup part-skim ricotta or chunky cottage cheese
3 egg whites
1 tablespoon fresh basil, chopped
1 teaspoon Tabasco
1/4 teaspoon nutmeg
fresh ground black pepper

Preheat the oven or grill. Mix the spinach, onion, garlic, mushrooms, and arti-chokes. Add one can of mushroom soup, parmesan cheese, mozzarella cheese, ricotta or cottage cheese, egg whites, basil, Tabasco, nutmeg, and black pepper.

Grease a small roasting pan or 9 x 13 casserole dish. Make a layer of 2 to 3 uncooked lasagna noodles, then a thin layer of the vegetable/cheese mixture, a layer of roast peppers, and another layer of the vegetable/cheese mixture. Finish building the lasagna with more pasta noodles and the second can of mushroom soup.

Cover and bake in a pre-heated oven or grill for 45 to 60 minutes. Uncover and bake for 10 to 15 minutes. Allow to rest for 10 minutes before serving.

NUTRITIONAL INFORMATION

CALORIES 360

PROTEIN	19 g	CHOLESTEROL	53 mg
FAT	8 g	FIBER	5 g
SAT. FAT	4 g	SODIUM	500 mg

Not all pasta requires a red sauce. This garlic sauce proves my point.

SCALLOPS & PASTA WITH GARLIC SAUCE

Makes 4 servings
Temperature: medium, then low

1 pound linguini, cooked al dente
1 pound scallops
1 head Caramelized Garlic (see page 104)
2 teaspoons sesame oil
1 red pepper, chopped
2 green onions, chopped
1 tablespoon ginger, chopped
2 tablespoon hoisin sauce
1 tablespoon light soy sauce
2 cups bok choy greens, chopped
1 cup chicken broth

Preheat a wok or large sauté pan on medium heat. Add the sesame oil, garlic, ginger, green onions, and scallops, and stir-fry for one minute.

Add the bok choy and red pepper, and stir-fry for a minute.

Combine the chicken broth, hoisin sauce, and soy sauce; add to the wok and cook on high heat for 2 minutes. Toss in the cooked pasta.

NUTRITIONAL INFORMATION

CALORIES 340

PROTEIN	28 g	CHOLESTEROL	45 mg
FAT	4.5 g	FIBER	5 g
SAT. FAT	1 g	SODIUM	660 mg

I keep individually wrapped boneless chicken breasts in the freezer. Then, when I'm in a rush to prepare a quick healthy dinner, I'll defrost them in the microwave while my grill heats up. Dinner is only 10 minutes away!

LEMON CHICKEN AND PASTA

Makes 4 servings
Temperature: grill medium, then low

1 pound cooked pasta such as penne or ziti
1 pound boneless chicken breasts, cut into strips
1 tablespoon olive oil
juice of 2 lemons
1 cup chicken broth
1 head Caramelized Garlic (see page 104)
1 tablespoon fresh basil, chopped
fresh ground black pepper
1/4 cup grated Parmigiano-Reggiano cheese
hot pepper flakes

Marinate the chicken in the lemon juice and olive oil for 30 minutes. Preheat the grill and a saucepan.

Grill the chicken breasts for 2 minutes on each side. Place the chicken in the saucepan. Add the garlic, chicken broth, basil, and black pepper. Simmer for several minutes until the chicken is fully cooked. Top with cheese and pepper flakes, then toss with the pasta.

NUTRITIONAL INFORMATION

CALORIES 380			
PROTEIN	34 g	CHOLESTEROL	38 mg
FAT	9 g	FIBER	2 g
SAT. FAT	3 g	SODIUM	370 mg

Orzo may look like a large grain of rice, but it's actually a pasta. As with all starches, the taste will be as good as the ingredients it is served with.

ORZO AND CARAMELIZED ONION

≈≈≈≈≈≈≈≈≈

Serves 4
Temperature: medium, then low

2 cups orzo, cooked
1 teaspoon olive oil
$^1/_4$ cup Caramelized Onion (see page 105)
1 cup fresh spinach
2 tablespoons pine nuts or walnuts
pinch nutmeg
fresh ground black pepper

Preheat a sauté pan. Add the olive oil, onion, and pine nuts or walnuts. Add the cooked orzo, nutmeg, and fresh ground black pepper. Cook for 4 to 5 minutes, or until the orzo is hot. Add the spinach and serve.

NUTRITIONAL INFORMATION

CALORIES 140			
PROTEIN	5 g	CHOLESTEROL	24 mg
FAT	2.5 g	FIBER	1 g
SAT. FAT	0 g	SODIUM	10 mg

Crab seems to lend itself well to being served with creamy foods. This pasta dish offers great flavor and a creamy texture, without the fat.

CREAMY CRAB PASTA

Serves 4
Temperature: medium

1 pound cooked rotelli or short twist pasta
1 cup blue, Dungeness, or snow crabmeat
1 cup nonfat ricotta cheese
1/2 cup part-skim mozzarella cheese
1 cup chicken broth
1/2 cup nonfat half-and-half
pinch nutmeg
1 teaspoon hot sauce
1 cup arugula, washed

Preheat a large saucepan. Add the chicken broth, half-and-half, nutmeg, and hot sauce. Warm slightly. Mix the crab with the cooked pasta, ricotta cheese, and mozzarella cheese, then combine with the warmed broth and half-and-half. Continue to heat until completely warm.

Mix in the arugula just before serving.

NUTRITIONAL INFORMATION

CALORIES 300

PROTEIN	24 g	CHOLESTEROL	41 mg
FAT	3.5 g	FIBER	2 g
SAT. FAT	1.5 g	SODIUM	310 mg

Having guests over for dinner? The eggplant and sauce can be prepared well in advance. Then just reheat, add the pasta, and dinner is ready!

RIGATONI AND EGGPLANT

Serves 4
Temperature: medium

1 pound rigatoni pasta, cooked
2 tablespoons olive oil
2 cups eggplant, peeled and chopped
1/2 cup onion, chopped
8 cloves Caramelized Garlic (see page 104)
6 plum tomatoes, deseeded and chopped
1 green bell pepper, chopped
1/4 cup green olives, chopped
1/2 cup white wine
1 cup chicken broth
1 teaspoon dried basil
1 teaspoon oregano
1 teaspoon thyme
1 teaspoon hot sauce
1 tablespoon pine nuts
1 tablespoon fresh basil

Preheat a large nonstick saucepan. Add the olive oil, eggplant, onion, garlic, tomatoes, and bell pepper. Cook until light brown. Add the wine, chicken broth, olives, dried basil, oregano, thyme, and hot sauce. Cook for 10 to 12 minutes; mix in the cooked rigatoni.

Top with fresh basil and pine nuts.

NUTRITIONAL INFORMATION

CALORIES 330			
PROTEIN	10 g	CHOLESTEROL	47 mg
FAT	10 g	FIBER	6 g
SAT. FAT	1.5 g	SODIUM	280 mg

A savory, slightly vinegary and sweet taste is not a typical accompaniment to pasta. Once you try this combination, however, you will always cook extra pork to make this recipe.

BBQ PORK AND LINGUINE

Serves 4
Temperature: medium, then low

1 pound lean pork, precooked or leftover, shredded or chopped fine
12 ounces linguine, cooked al dente
1/2 cup onion, chopped
1 tablespoon olive oil
8 cloves Caramelized Garlic (see page 104)
1 green bell pepper, chopped
6 plum tomatoes, deseeded and chopped
1 cup white beans, cooked or canned
1 cup tomato sauce
2 tablespoons vinegar
1 tablespoon honey
1 teaspoon rosemary
1 teaspoon hot sauce

Preheat a large saucepan. Add the olive oil, onion, and garlic. Allow to cook, stirring occasionally until light brown. Add the green bell pepper, tomatoes, and pork; cook for 2 to 3 minutes. Add the beans, tomato sauce, vinegar, honey, rosemary, and hot sauce. Cook for 20 to 30 minutes, then mix in hot cooked linguine.

NUTRITIONAL INFORMATION

CALORIES 350

PROTEIN	40 g	CHOLESTEROL	29 mg
FAT	9 g	FIBER	3 g
SAT. FAT	3 g	SODIUM	430 mg

I am always asked where my recipes come from. Most of the recipes are developed as I think of a particular food. However, occasionally I am amazed at the tastes of very simply prepared dishes. Usually they will come from my family, friends, or, in this case, a very special person from a very special childhood memory.

MOCK CHOP SUEY

Makes 6 servings
Temperature: medium, then low

1 pound elbow macaroni pasta
1 pound ground sirloin beef, 90% lean, or lean ground turkey
2 bell peppers, split, seeded, and chopped
1/2 cup onion, chopped
2 cups canned whole plum tomatoes and juice, chopped

Preheat a large nonstick saucepan. Add the ground beef and brown. Drain off all the fat; add the peppers and onion. Cook for 4 to 5 minutes, then add the tomatoes. Simmer for 30 minutes.

Boil elbow pasta until al dente, drain, and mix with the meat sauce. Simmer for a minute, then serve.

NUTRITIONAL INFORMATION

CALORIES 250

PROTEIN	18 g	CHOLESTEROL	28 mg
FAT	7 g	FIBER	2 g
SAT. FAT	2 g	SODIUM	80 mg

A low fat turkey sausage will cut down the fat grams in this recipe. Don't tell anyone the sausage is low fat—they'll think it's the real magilla.

TOMATO RICE WITH SMOKED SAUSAGE

Makes 4 servings
Temperature: grill medium, then low

1 cup raw rice
2 cups reduced sodium chicken broth
6 plum tomatoes, split and grilled
1/4 onion, sliced and grilled
6 cloves Caramelized Garlic (see page 104)
1 pound low fat smoked turkey sausage, grilled and sliced
1 teaspoon Tabasco

Preheat a saucepan on the grill or side burner.

Add the rice, chicken broth, tomatoes, onion, garlic, and Tabasco in a pot. Simmer for 15 minutes. Add the grilled smoked turkey sausage.

Cook for 10 minutes or until done. Serve.

NOTE: To lower the high sodium content, substitute regular or hot sausage for the smoked sausage.

NUTRITIONAL INFORMATION

CALORIES 390			
PROTEIN	22 g	CHOLESTEROL	49 mg
FAT	11 g	FIBER	2 g
SAT. FAT	3 g	SODIUM	1280 mg

This recipe can be made in minutes. Serve it hot or cold as a pasta salad.

FETTUCINE WITH ASPARAGUS AND SUNDRIED TOMATO DRESSING

Makes 6 servings

1^1/2 pounds fettucine, cooked
1 bunch fresh asparagus, separate stems and tips and blanch individually
^{1}/2 cup sliced black olives
6 cloves Caramelized Garlic (see page 104)
^{1}/4 cup plum tomatoes, chopped
^{1}/2 cup Italian Dressing (see page 78)
3 tablespoons grated parmesan cheese
1 tablespoon fresh basil, chopped
fresh ground black pepper

Precook the pasta and asparagus stems and tips separately, then cool. Toss the fettucine with the cooked asparagus stems, olives, garlic, tomatoes, and dressing. Add the parmesan cheese, basil, and fresh ground black pepper. Top the pasta with the cooked asparagus tips.

NUTRITIONAL INFORMATION

CALORIES 250			
PROTEIN	9 g	CHOLESTEROL	38 mg
FAT	8 g	FIBER	17 g
SAT. FAT	1.5 g	SODIUM	320 mg

PAELLA RICE

Makes 6 servings
Temperature: high, then low

2 tablespoons olive oil
2 cups long-grain brown rice or arborio rice
1 red or green bell pepper, chopped
4 plum tomatoes, coarsely chopped
6 cloves Caramelized Garlic (see page 104)
1 teaspoon paprika
4 cups hot chicken broth
1 teaspoon Tabasco
1/2 teaspoon saffron threads, or 1 teaspoon turmeric
1 cup cooked chickpeas
1/2 cup grean peas, fresh or frozen
1/4 cup sliced green or black olives
2 green onions or scallions, chopped
1 pound grilled chicken, seafood, or turkey burgers (optional)

Preheat a paella or large sauté pan with a tight-fitting cover. Heat the olive oil in the pan, then add the rice, pepper, tomato, garlic, and paprika. Stirring constantly, cook for 2 minutes, or until the rice is lightly toasted. Add the broth, Tabasco, and saffron or turmeric and bring to a boil, then lower the heat.

Simmer for 5 minutes. Add the chickpeas, green peas, olives, and green onions or scallions, and cook until the rice is tender—about 5 minutes.

Add the chicken, seafood, or grilled turkey burgers, if desired. Remove from the heat and set aside for 5 minutes before serving.

NUTRITIONAL INFORMATION

CALORIES 580

PROTEIN	19 g	CHOLESTEROL	0 mg
FAT	12 g	FIBER	8 g
SAT. FAT	2 g	SODIUM	890 mg

VEGETABLES

CARAMELIZED GARLIC

Makes 6 heads
Temperature: grill low or 325°F oven

6 heads fresh garlic
2 tablespoons olive oil
12-inch square of aluminum foil

Lay each garlic head on its side and cut off $^1/_4$ inch from the bottom or root end, exposing the garlic cloves. Brush with olive oil. Place the heads, exposed end down, in a single layer in an ovenproof dish or directly on the grill. Roast in a 325° oven or on a very low grill, uncovered, until light brown. Cover with aluminum foil and cook 8 to 10 minutes longer, or until creamy.

Allow the garlic to cool. Remove the clove from the head as needed. Garlic may be stored in a tightly covered container in the refrigerator for several days.

To puree, crush garlic cloves with the flat of a knife.

NUTRITIONAL INFORMATION
(PER CLOVE)

CALORIES 5			
PROTEIN	0 g	CHOLESTEROL	1 mg
FAT	0 g	FIBER	0 g
SAT. FAT	0 g	SODIUM	0 mg

WHY CARAMELIZE GARLIC?
Because it's all in the flavor—and that's what cooking and eating is all about. Raw garlic, just like raw onions, are bitter and can have a biting affect on the palate. However, once roasted, the natural sugars in garlic brown and become full of sweetness. This golden caramelized layer on the outside of the garlic clove contains a sweet and robust taste that will complement any foods that call for this bulb. Make several heads at a time. Keep extra heads handy in refrigerator to use in all recipes, and use as a substitute for butter on bread!

It doesn't get any sweeter than this! Try using Vidalia, Texas, Maui, or Walla Walla onions for an added zing of sweetness.

CARAMELIZED ONIONS

Makes 1 cup
Temperature: medium then low

2 cups onion, sliced

Preheat a saucepan to a medium heat. Place the onions in the pan and cover. Allow to cook for 2 to 3 minutes, or until the onions begin to brown. Stir and cover again. Continue the process until the onions are a golden brown. Remove the cover. Cook off any excess moisture. Remove the onions from the pan and cool.

NUTRITIONAL INFORMATION

CALORIES 80

PROTEIN	3 g	CHOLESTEROL	15 mg
FAT	1 g	FIBER	2 g
SAT. FAT	0 g	SODIUM	25 mg

These large, meaty mushroom caps are ideal for stuffing. They make an ideal appetizer or luncheon dish and are a very satisfying nonmeat alternative.

PORTOBELLO MUSHROOMS WITH SPINACH STUFFING

Makes 4 servings
Temperature: grill high to medium, or 350°F oven

4 3-inch Portobello mushrooms, stems removed
2 tablespoons olive oil
8 cloves Caramelized Garlic (see page 104)
2 cups spinach, cooked, with excess liquid removed
1/4 cup toasted pineapple, chopped
pinch nutmeg
pinch allspice
1 teaspoon hot sauce

Preheat the grill or oven to 350°F. If using an oven, place the mushrooms gill side up on a nonstick pan sprayed with oil.

Mix the spinach, olive oil, garlic, pineapple, nutmeg, allspice, and hot sauce. Divide the spinach filling among the four mushroom caps. Cook on the grill for 2 minutes on high, then move to the low side for 8 to 10 minutes—or bake in the oven for 10 to 12 minutes.

NUTRITIONAL INFORMATION

CALORIES 120

PROTEIN	7 g	CHOLESTEROL	12 mg
FAT	7 g	FIBER	6 g
SAT. FAT	1 g	SODIUM	75 mg

This vegetable chili can make a great appetizer, side dish, or a complete meal. If you must, you can add meat, chicken, or seafood to change the flavor.

VEGETABLE CHILI

Serves 6

2 tablespoons olive oil
^{1}/2 cup onion, chopped
8 cloves Caramelized Garlic (see page 104)
3 green onions, chopped
1 cup zucchini, diced
1 cup yellow squash, diced
1 cup eggplant, peeled and diced
1^1/2 cups white beans, cooked
1 sweet potato, peeled and diced
2 teaspoons cumin
1 teaspoon basil
1 teaspoon oregano
1 teaspoon thyme
2 cups chicken or vegetable broth
2 teaspoons hot sauce
1 tablespoon cilantro, chopped

Preheat a large soup pot. Add the olive oil. Add the onion and garlic and cook until light brown. Toss in the green onions, zucchini, yellow squash, eggplant, and sweet potato. Cook for 2 minutes, stirring occasionally, then add the cumin, basil, oregano, and thyme. Add the beans, chicken or vegetable broth, hot sauce, and cilantro. Simmer for 20 to 25 minutes.

NOTE: Do not overcook this chili, to maintain the maximum amount of nutritional content. Prepare a day in advance to increase the flavor.

NUTRITIONAL INFORMATION

CALORIES 160

PROTEIN	5 g	CHOLESTEROL	22 mg
FAT	6 g	FIBER	2 g
SAT. FAT	1 g	SODIUM	270 mg

This is a very quick salad or side dish to make—you don't even need a knife!
Make it a few hours ahead of time to allow the flavors to blend together.

HOMINY, CORN, AND PEA SALAD

Serves 4

1 cup hominy, canned
1/2 cup sweet peas, canned
1 cup corn, canned
1 teaspoon cider vinegar
1 teaspoon ketchup
1 teaspoon honey
1/2 teaspoon cumin
1 teaspoon fresh cilantro
juice from 1 fresh lime

Mix the hominy, sweet peas, corn, vinegar, ketchup, honey, cumin, cilantro, and lime juice.

Refrigerate until ready to serve.

NUTRITIONAL INFORMATION

CALORIES 70

PROTEIN	2 g	CHOLESTEROL	16 mg
FAT	0.5 g	FIBER	2 g
SAT. FAT	0 g	SODIUM	180 mg

Prepare this dish ahead of time to allow the flavors to improve. Making extra will give you a handy side dish to eat when you need a quick, nutritious snack.

EGGPLANT & OLIVES

Makes 4 servings
Temperature: grill high to medium

1 medium eggplant, peeled and sliced
2 tablespoons olive oil
1 teaspoon basil
$^{1}/_{4}$ cup cured olives, pitted
8 cloves Caramelized Garlic (see page 104)
$^{1}/_{2}$ teaspoon hot pepper flakes

Preheat the grill.

Grill the eggplant until a light brown. Cool and mix with the olive oil, basil, olives, garlic, and hot pepper flakes.

NUTRITIONAL INFORMATION

CALORIES 110			
PROTEIN	2 g	CHOLESTEROL	9 mg
FAT	8 g	FIBER	3 g
SAT. FAT	1 g	SODIUM	75 mg

I like serving the carrots and red peppers with a number of different dishes. The bright orange and red look very nice with other foods. When I need to prepare some dishes ahead of time, the carrots will withstand any type of delay without losing color, texture, or taste.

CARROTS AND RED PEPPERS

Makes 4 servings
Temperature: medium, then low

2 cups shredded carrots
1 red bell pepper, cut into fine strips
2 cloves Caramelized Garlic (see page 104)
1 cup apple juice
1/2 teaspoon cumin
1 teaspoon cilantro, chopped
fresh ground black pepper

Heat the apple juice in a small saucepan. Add the carrots, red pepper, garlic, cumin, cilantro, and black pepper. Simmer for 10 to 12 minutes, or until the carrots become slightly tender.

NUTRITIONAL INFORMATION

CALORIES 60

PROTEIN	1 g	CHOLESTEROL	15 mg
FAT	0 g	FIBER	2 g
SAT. FAT	0 g	SODIUM	20 mg

When choosing fats, those found in olives and nuts are good choices. The walnuts also add a nice contrast of crunch to the soft spinach.

SPINACH AND WALNUTS

Serves 2
Temperature: medium

8 cups ($^1/_2$ pound) fresh spinach, cleaned
1 tablespoon olive oil
$^1/_4$ cup chopped walnuts, toasted
fresh ground black pepper

Preheat a large sauté pan. Add the olive oil, toss in spinach that is slightly wet, and cover for a minute. Top with toasted walnuts and fresh ground black pepper. Serve immediately.

NUTRITIONAL INFORMATION

CALORIES 90

PROTEIN	4 g	CHOLESTEROL	3 mg
FAT	8 g	FIBER	2 g
SAT. FAT	1 g	SODIUM	45 mg

Preparation time is saved by not peeling the potatoes. By keeping the skins on, you'll also be serving the potatoes with added minerals and fiber.

POTATO SMASH

Makes 6 servings
Temperature: medium then low

3 cups red new potatoes, washed and chopped
¹/₄ cup Caramelized Onion (see page 105)
6 cloves Caramelized Garlic (see page 104)
¹/₄ cup fat free cheddar cheese, shredded
¹/₄ cup plain low fat yogurt
¹/₄ cup fat free half-and-half, warmed
1 green onion, chopped
¹/₄ teaspoon nutmeg
1 teaspoon Tabasco
fresh ground black pepper

Place the potatoes in a pot, cover with cold water, and bring to a boil. Simmer about 15 to 20 minutes, or until the potatoes are tender; drain well. Mash the potatoes, then add the onion, garlic, cheese, yogurt, half-and-half, green onion, nutmeg, Tabasco, and black pepper. Mix well.

NUTRITIONAL INFORMATION

CALORIES 90

PROTEIN	4 g	CHOLESTEROL	17 mg
FAT	0.5 g	FIBER	1 g
SAT. FAT	0 g	SODIUM	15 mg

Potatoes are rich in vitamin C, B6, potassium, and other minerals. There's no guilt with this stuffed version. You'll have plenty of long-range energy from the complex carbohydrates.

DOUBLE-BAKED POTATOES

Makes 4 servings
Temperature: medium grill or 350°F oven

6 baking potatoes, well scrubbed
1 red pepper—split, seeded, roasted or grilled, then chopped
1/2 cup canned creamed corn
1/4 cup low fat mozzarella cheese, shredded
2 tablespoons plain low fat yogurt
1 teaspoon Tabasco
pinch nutmeg
fresh ground black pepper
2 tablespoons bread crumbs

Preheat the oven. Bake six potatoes until done, then let them cool.

Smash two potatoes with the skins on. Take the remaining four potatoes and hollow out the centers. Set the skins aside. Add to the smashed potatoes. Mix in the red pepper, corn, mozzarella cheese, yogurt, Tabasco, nutmeg, and black pepper.

Fill the four potato skins with the mix. Sprinkle bread crumbs on top. Bake for 15 to 20 minutes until hot and light brown on top.

NUTRITIONAL INFORMATION

CALORIES 267			
PROTEIN	7 g	CHOLESTEROL	57 mg
FAT	2 g	FIBER	6 g
SAT. FAT	1 g	SODIUM	90 mg

Rutabagas are great to keep in the pantry during the cooler months. Unlike other highly perishable vegetables, the rutabaga stays fresh longer.

RUTABAGA & CARAMELIZED ONION

Makes 6 servings
Temperature: grill medium then low, or 350°F oven

1 large rutabaga, peeled and cubed
1/2 cup Caramlized Onion (see page 105)
2 green apples, cored and cubed very small
juice of a lemon
pinch of nutmeg
fresh ground black pepper
vegetable spray

Place the rutabaga in a pot and bring to a boil; simmer until slightly tender. While the rutabaga is simmering, spray a nonstick ovenproof pan with vegetable spray. Place the apples and lemon juice in the pan.

Drain the rutabaga well, then add immediately to the apples. Mix in the onion, nutmeg, and fresh ground black pepper.

Bake for 8 to 10 minutes, then serve.

NUTRITIONAL INFORMATION

CALORIES 60

PROTEIN	1 g	CHOLESTEROL	16 mg
FAT	0 g	FIBER	3 g
SAT. FAT	0 g	SODIUM	15 mg

Asparagus is like chicken—it can be prepared in a variety of ways and will always taste great. Be sure, however, not to overcook.

ASPARAGUS AND PEANUTS

Makes 4 servings
Temperature: medium

2 cups asparagus, boiled al dente and chopped
1 teaspoon sesame oil
3 cloves Caramalized Garlic (see page 104)
2 tablespoons unsalted peanuts, chopped
1 teaspoon light soy sauce

Preheat a nonstick sauté pan. Add sesame oil, garlic, peanuts, asparagus, and soy sauce. Sauté for 2 minutes, stirring occasionally.

NUTRITIONAL INFORMATION

CALORIES 50

PROTEIN	3 g	CHOLESTEROL	5 mg
FAT	3.5 g	FIBER	2 g
SAT. FAT	0 g	SODIUM	45 mg

Foods "con queso" are usually loaded in fat, but since I enjoy foods with cheese, a good compromise is a lower fat version. This recipe requires only a few ingredients and can be made in a short amount of time.

GREEN BEANS CON QUESO

Makes 6 servings
Temperature: low

1 pound green beans, cooked or frozen cut into 2-inch pieces
1/2 cup low fat cheddar cheese
4 ounces fat free cream cheese
1/4 cup fat free half-and-half
1 cup salsa

In a large saucepan combine the cheddar cheese, cream cheese, and half-and-half. Heat the mixture very slowly, stirring constantly. Add the beans, and mix in the salsa as the beans become hot.

NUTRITIONAL INFORMATION

CALORIES 80

PROTEIN	7 g	CHOLESTEROL	11 mg
FAT	1 g	FIBER	3 g
SAT. FAT	0 g	SODIUM	260 mg

Brussels sprouts have always been one of my favorite vegetables. I enjoy their taste and texture. Or maybe I'm just taken with their mini-cabbage appearance!

SWEET & SOUR BRUSSELS SPROUTS

≈≈≈≈≈≈≈≈

Makes 6 servings
Temperature: low

1 pint brussels sprouts, washed and trimmed
¹/₄ cup Caramelized Onion (see page 105)
4 cloves Caramelized Garlic (see page 104)
¹/₄ cup pineapple chunks
¹/₄ cup pineapple juice
1 tablespoon apple cider vinegar
1 tablespoon ketchup
1 teaspoon lite soy sauce
1 teaspoon Tabasco

Remove any dark outer leaves from the brussels sprouts, trim off the stem ends, and cut an X in the ends with a sharp knife. Add to boiling water until tender but al dente and drain.

In a sauté pan add the onion, garlic, pineapple chunks, pineapple juice, vinegar, ketchup, soy sauce, and Tabasco. Heat until warm. Add the brussels sprouts and cook for 2 minutes.

NUTRITIONAL INFORMATION

CALORIES 50

PROTEIN	3 g	CHOLESTEROL	12 mg
FAT	0 g	FIBER	3 g
SAT. FAT	0 g	SODIUM	110 mg

The white cousin to broccoli, cauliflower is a great source of vitamin C, high in fiber, and low in calories.

CAULIFLOWER WITH TOMATOES

Makes 6 servings
Temperature: medium then low

2 cups cauliflower florets, cooked
6 plum tomatoes, split
1 teaspoon olive oil
2 green onions
$^1/_4$ cup green olives
juice of a lemon
1 teaspoon oregano
1 teaspoon Tabasco
pinch of nutmeg
fresh ground black pepper

Preheat a nonstick sauté pan. Add the olive oil and green onion and sauté for a minute. Add the cauliflower, oregano, lemon, Tabasco, nutmeg, and black pepper. Cook for 2 minutes and serve.

NUTRITIONAL INFORMATION

CALORIES 35			
PROTEIN	1 g	CHOLESTEROL	7 mg
FAT	1 g	FIBER	2 g
SAT. FAT	0 g	SODIUM	65 mg

When my garden starts pumping out the zucchini, I will prepare a different recipe each day. Here is my recipe from Tuesday.

SQUASH BAKE

4 cups zucchini, sliced and grilled
2 tablespoons whole grain flour
$^1/_4$ cup Carmelized Onion (see page 105)
2 cups fat free milk
$^1/_2$ cup egg substitute
$^1/_4$ cup feta cheese, crumbled
$^1/_2$ teaspoon oregano
1 teaspoon Tabasco
pinch of nutmeg
vegetable spray
$^1/_2$ cup whole wheat fresh bread crumbs

Preheat the oven. Spray a nonstick tart or casserole pan with vegetable spray. Place the bread crumbs on the bottom of the dish. Mix the flour with the grilled zucchini and layer with the caramelized onion.

Mix the milk with the egg substitute, oregano, Tabasco, and nutmeg. Pour the egg and milk mixture over the zucchini. Top with the feta cheese. Bake for 25 to 30 minutes or until set.

NUTRITIONAL INFORMATION

CALORIES 90

PROTEIN	8 g	CHOLESTEROL	10 g
FAT	2.5 g	FIBER	1 g
SAT. FAT	1 g	SODIUM	170 g

Who says you can't get great taste out of a vegetable?

VEGETABLE ROAST

Serves 4
Temperature: grill medium, or 350°F oven

1/2 cup onions, cut into finger-size pieces
1/2 cup carrots, cut into finger-size pieces
1/2 cup peppers, yellow, red, and/or green, cut into finger-size pieces
1/2 cup eggplant, cut into finger-size pieces
1/2 cup sweet potato, cut into finger-size pieces
6 cloves Caramelized Garlic (see page 104)
1 teaspoon rosemary
1 teaspoon thyme
1/2 teaspoon Tabasco
2 tablespoons olive oil
fresh ground black pepper

Preheat the oven or grill. Toss together the onion, carrots, peppers, eggplant, sweet potato, garlic, rosemary, thyme, Tabasco, olive oil, and fresh ground black pepper.

Place in an ovenproof roasting pan. Roast for 45 minutes, turning every 10 to 15 minutes as the vegetables begin to brown.

NUTRITIONAL INFORMATION

CALORIES 120

PROTEIN	1 g	CHOLESTEROL	13 mg
FAT	7 g	FIBER	2 g
SAT. FAT	1 g	SODIUM	15 mg

It may be a play on the old BLT—bacon, lettuce, and tomato sandwich—but no one will complain with this low fat, complex-carb sandwich. It will keep them fueled all afternoon!

VLT (VEGETABLE, LETTUCE, & TOMATO)

Makes 4 servings

1 large whole grain baguette bread loaf, split lengthwise
4 slices eggplant, peeled, sliced and grilled
2 red bell peppers, split, deseeded, and grilled
4 slices zucchini, sliced thin lengthwise and grilled
1 grilled Portobello mushroom, sliced
1 beefsteak or vine-ripened tomato, sliced
4 lettuce leaves, iceberg or other leaf lettuce
2 tablespoons Sandwich Spread (see page 85)

Layer the bread with the grilled eggplant, peppers, zucchini, and mushrooms. Add Sandwich Spread to one side of the bread. Top with lettuce and tomato, close the bread, and cut into four sandwiches.

NUTRITIONAL INFORMATION

CALORIES 330

PROTEIN	14 g	CHOLESTEROL	64 mg
FAT	5 g	FIBER	12 g
SAT. FAT	1 g	SODIUM	610 mg

If you missed that glass of orange juice this morning, shame on you. But don't feel too bad about it—have a cup of broccoli and make up the vitamin C.

BROCCOLI IN TOMATO BROTH

~~~~~~~~~~~~~~~~~~~~

Makes 4 servings
Temperature: high then low

1 bunch broccoli, stems cut and peeled
1 cup tomato sauce
4 cloves Caramelized Garlic (see page 104)
1 tablespoon fresh basil, chopped
1 teaspoon Tabasco
juice of a lemon
fresh ground black pepper

In a saucepan, heat the tomato sauce with the garlic, basil, Tabasco, lemon, and black pepper.

Fill a large soup pot with water and bring to a boil. Add the broccoli and cook for a minute in the rapidly boiling water. Drain and add the broccoli to the tomato broth.

NUTRITIONAL INFORMATION

CALORIES 50			
PROTEIN	3 g	CHOLESTEROL	12 mg
FAT	0 g	FIBER	3 g
SAT. FAT	0 g	SODIUM	400 mg

Broccoli is also an excellent source of fiber and low in calories. It doesn't end there, though, because you'll also receive vitamin A, folate, calcium, iron, protein, bioflavinoids, and other plant chemicals that protect against cancer. When served with the tomato broth, it also tastes great!

There are never enough ways to prepare zucchini when my garden is pumping them out. I prepare this recipe for my Southwest feast.

ZUCCHINI WITH CILANTRO PESTO

Makes 4 servings
Temperature: high then medium

2 medium zucchini squash, sliced into small pieces
1 tablespoon olive oil
2 tablespoons Cilantro Pesto (see page 168)

Preheat the sauté pan. Brush olive oil on the zucchini. Place the zucchini in a hot pan and sauté quickly until the zucchini is slightly tender. Toss in Cilantro Pesto and serve.

NUTRITIONAL INFORMATION

CALORIES 70			
PROTEIN	2 g	CHOLESTEROL	4 mg
FAT	5 g	FIBER	1 g
SAT. FAT	0.5 g	SODIUM	50 mg

Any hot or sweet peppers can be used if fresh jalapeños keep you awake at night.

JALAPEÑO POTATOES

Makes 6 servings
Temperature: medium

6 medium baking potatoes, boiled or baked, cut into wedges
2 tablespoons olive oil
6 cloves Caramelized Garlic (see page 104)
4 jalapeños, seeded and chopped
1 red bell pepper, seeded and chopped
1 tablespoon cilantro, rough chopped
1 teaspoon paprika
$^1/_2$ teaspoon ground nutmeg
fresh ground black pepper

Preheat a cast-iron skillet or nonstick sauté pan on medium heat. Add the olive oil, garlic, jalapeños, red peppers, and potatoes. Season with cilantro, paprika, nutmeg, and black pepper. Turn when the potatoes begin to brown. Continue cooking until the potatoes are hot and brown all over.

NUTRITIONAL INFORMATION

CALORIES 190

PROTEIN	3 g	CHOLESTEROL	35 mg
FAT	5 g	FIBER	3 g
SAT. FAT	0.5 g	SODIUM	10 mg

Broccoli rabe is a variety of broccoli with small heads and pleasantly bitter leaves. It can be made as a vegetable, as an ingredient in pasta or in salads, and as below. You will soon develop a liking for it and see what the fuss is all about. Just don't tell anyone on how good it is for you.

BROCCOLI RABE

Makes 4 servings
Temperature: medium

1 bunch broccoli rabe (about 1 pound)
2 tablespoons olive oil
6 cloves Caramelized Garlic (see page 104)
1/2 cup chicken broth
1 tablespoon lite soy sauce
1 teaspoon Tabasco
2 tablespoons unsalted peanuts, toasted and chopped

Wash the broccoli rabe in water and peel the stems if they are very thick.

Preheat a sauté pan. Add the olive oil and garlic, and cook for 1 minute. Add the broccoli rabe and chicken broth.

Cover and cook for 10 minutes, or until the broccoli rabe becomes tender. Season with soy sauce and Tabasco and top with unsalted peanuts.

NUTRITIONAL INFORMATION

CALORIES 120			
PROTEIN	5 g	CHOLESTEROL	6 mg
FAT	9 g	FIBER	1 g
SAT. FAT	1 g	SODIUM	130 mg

The only better way to make this corn is to haul your grill out into the corn-field!

CORN ROAST

Makes 6 servings
Ttemperature: grill medium, then low

6 ears fresh corn
2 tablespoons olive oil
1 head Caramelized Garlic (see page 104)
1 medium onion, sliced thin
3 slices low fat bacon or turkey bacon, cut in half
pinch of ground nutmeg
1 teaspoon fresh ground black pepper

Pull the corn husks back, but do not remove them. Remove and discard the corn silk. Soak the whole cobs in a pot of cold water for 15 minutes. Remove the corn from the water.

Preheat the grill.

Brush the corn with the olive oil and rub with the garlic. Place the onion and the bacon inside the husks, then season with nutmeg and black pepper. Reposition the corn husks over the kernels and tie each ear with a piece of the husk or twine. Place on the grill on medium heat, turning every 2 minutes. After 7 or 8 minutes, place on indirect heat or on a top shelf. Total cooking time is 25 to 30 minutes.

NOTE: When preparing a large amount of corn, you can wrap the ears in foil.

NUTRITIONAL INFORMATION

CALORIES 150

PROTEIN	5 g	CHOLESTEROL	21 mg
FAT	7 g	FIBER	3 g
SAT. FAT	1 g	SODIUM	105 mg

Eggplant can rule the vegetable world on the grill. Some people I know will only eat it grilled, although this recipe tastes equally well baked in an oven.

STUFFED EGGPLANT

Makes 6 servings
Temperature: grill medium then low; or 400°F oven, then 325°

2 medium-size eggplants, peeled and thinly sliced lengthwise
3 tablespoons olive oil
1 cup low fat ricotta cheese
3 tablespoons grated parmesan cheese
1 cup low fat mozzarella, shredded
6 cloves Caramelized Garlic (see page 104)
1 tablespoon fresh basil, chopped
pinch of ground nutmeg
1/4 cup Italian flavored croutons
1 egg substitute

Preheat the grill or oven.

Brush the eggplant slices with olive oil and grill or bake each side until lightly browned and soft. Remove and cool.

In a medium bowl combine the ricotta, parmesan, mozzarella, garlic, basil, nutmeg, croutons, and egg substitute.

Place 2 tablespoons of the cheese mixture in the middle of a slice of eggplant. Roll the ends up over the filling and place the eggplant in a nonstick pan.

Bake at 325°F for 25 minutes. Serve as is or top with your favorite tomato sauce.

NUTRITIONAL INFORMATION

CALORIES 230			
PROTEIN	14 g	CHOLESTEROL	16 mg
FAT	13 g	FIBER	4 g
SAT. FAT	5 g	SODIUM	320 mg

Swiss chard reminds us that not everything in life is sweet. However, when partnered with the Sweet Potatoes and Marshmallows recipe (on page 127), the flavors are wonderfully balanced.

SWISS CHARD

Makes 6 servings
Temperature: grill medium then low

1 bunch red Swiss chard, washed, stems trimmed and chopped
1 cup Caramelized Onions (see page 103)
1 tablespoon cider vinegar
1/4 cup orange juice
1/2 teaspoon Tabasco
fresh ground black pepper

Preheat a sauté pan on the grill or side burner. Add the orange juice, vinegar, Tabasco, and Swiss chard stems. Simmer for 2 minutes. Add the chopped Swiss chard leaves. Cook for 2 minutes. Add the onions and ground black pepper to taste.

NUTRITIONAL INFORMATION

CALORIES 30			
PROTEIN	2 g	CHOLESTEROL	7 mg
FAT	0 g	FIBER	3 g
SAT. FAT	0 g	SODIUM	120 mg

This tasty and nutritious vegetable recipe is so yummy it may be mistaken for a dessert. If the kids think so, then let them. (Even the big kids!)

SWEET POTATOES AND MARSH-MALLOWS

Makes 4 servings
Temperature: grill medium or 375°F oven

4 large sweet potatoes (about 2¹/2 pounds), scrubbed
   (if cooking on the grill, wrap in foil)
¹/2 cup mini marshmallows
2 tablespoons low fat margarine
4 tablespoons orange juice
2 tablespoons brown sugar
¹/2 teaspoon cinnamon
pinch of ground nutmeg

Preheat the grill or oven. Place the foil-wrapped potatoes on the grill and bake for 30 to 40 minutes, depending on their size, turning occasionally. Remove when they're still a bit firm when pierced with a sharp knife.

Remove from the foil, then split the potatoes in half lengthwise. Scoop out half of the sweet potato pulp from each potato half. Divide the marshmallows evenly among the potato halves. Combine the margarine, orange juice, brown sugar, cinnamon, and nutmeg, and divide equally in the potato halves. Replace the scooped sweet potato back on top of the marshmallow mixture. Return the sweet potatoes to the grill for 5 minutes, or until the marshmallows melt.

NUTRITIONAL INFORMATION

CALORIES 250			
PROTEIN	3 g	CHOLESTEROL	55 mg
FAT	3 g	FIBER	5 g
SAT. FAT	0.5 g	SODIUM	55 mg

MEAT

The natural sweetness of the raisins in this dish will cool off the sting of the hot peppers. If there aren't any hot peppers in the pantry, steam sliced bell peppers in vinegar with hot pepper flakes.

PORK LOIN ROAST WITH HOT CHERRY PEPPERS

Makes 6 to 8 servings
Temperature: grill medium, then low, or 350°F oven

3¹/₂-pound boneless pork loin roast, boneless
1 head Caramelized Garlic (see page 104)
¹/₄ cup Pork Spice Blend (see page 163)
2 tablespoons cider vinegar
1 cup chicken broth
¹/₂ cup steak sauce
12 hot cherry or vinegar peppers; optional sweet peppers can be used
¹/₄ cup raisins

Rub the pork loin with the garlic and Pork Spice Blend and refrigerate overnight.

Preheat the grill or oven. Place the pork loin on the grill and lightly brown on all sides (or place in a roasting pan and cook for 30 minutes until brown). Lower the temperature and cook for 30 minutes, turning every 10 minutes on each side.

Preheat a medium saucepan on the grill or side burner. Add the vinegar, chicken broth, steak sauce, peppers and raisins. Heat to a boil, then lower the temperature to a simmer. Place the pork loin in the pan, cover, and cook slowly for 1 hour, or until fully cooked. The internal temperature should be 160° when checked with an instant-read thermometer.

Remove the meat from the pan and allow to cool for 20 minutes. Slice and serve with the juices.

NUTRITIONAL INFORMATION

CALORIES 330

PROTEIN	42 g	CHOLESTEROL	7 mg
FAT	14 g	FIBER	3 g
SAT. FAT	5 g	SODIUM	240 mg

It must be our primal nature to want to cook foods on a stick. It's fun, quick, and easy to prepare. This "sticky situation" is one worth repeating!

SEARED BEEF ON A STICK

Makes 4 servings
Temperature: grill high, then medium

1¹/₂ **pounds beef top round or flank, sliced in long thin strips 1¹/₂ inches wide**
1 **cup pineapple juice**
4 **cloves Caramelized Garlic (see page 104)**
2 **tablespoons honey**
1 **teaspoon hot pepper flakes**

Thread the beef strips on skewers. In a small bowl combine the pineapple juice, garlic, honey, and hot pepper flakes. Pour over the beef strips and marinate in the refrigerator for 2 hours.

Preheat the grill.

Place the skewered meat on high heat on the grill for 2 minutes on each side. Lower to a medium temperature and cook to desired doneness. Brush the beef with all the marinade.

NUTRITIONAL INFORMATION

CALORIES 300

PROTEIN	36 g	CHOLESTEROL	8 mg
FAT	13 g	FIBER	0 g
SAT. FAT	6 g	SODIUM	110 mg

Pork tenderloins have become increasing popular today. The versatility the tenderloins offer when combined with other foods makes it easy to prepare tasty dishes. Here the orzo helps trap all the flavorful pork juices.

PORK TENDERLOIN AND ORZO

Makes 4 servings
Temperature: grill high, then medium

1 12-ounce pork tenderloin
1 cup Pork Tenderloin Marinade (see page 162)
2 cups orzo, cooked
1 tablespoon cilantro

Trim any fat from the pork tenderloins and remove the silver skin. Add the trimmed pork tenderloin to the marinade. Marinate the pork overnight or for at least 2 hours in the refrigerator.

Preheat the grill.

Remove the pork tenderloins from the marinade and place on the grill. Sear on each side over high heat, about 2 minutes per side. Move the meat to medium heat and continue cooking for 8 to 10 minutes or until fully cooked, basting occasionally with the leftover marinade.

Remove from the grill and set the meat aside for 5 minutes before cutting. Slice thinly, toss with the orzo, and top with cilantro.

NUTRITIONAL INFORMATION

CALORIES 250

PROTEIN	22 g	CHOLESTEROL	24 mg
FAT	7 g	FIBER	1 g
SAT. FAT	1.5 g	SODIUM	80 mg

Using a lean pork tenderloin will reduce the fat from the canned version of pork and beans.

PORK AND BEANS

Makes 6 servings
Temperature: grill high, then low

1 8- to 10-ounce pork tenderloin
2 tablespoons Pork Spice Blend (see page 163)
1 teaspoon olive oil
8 cloves Caramelized Garlic (see page 104)
^{1}/2 cup onion, chopped
2 cups cooked red beans
1 cup tomato sauce
2 tablespoons cider vinegar
1 tablespoon honey
1 tablespoon brown sugar
1 teaspoon Tabasco

Trim any fat from the tenderloin and remove the silver skin. Cover the pork on all sides with the dry rub and refrigerate overnight or for 2 hours.

Preheat the grill.

Place the tenderloins on the grill and sear on all sides over high heat, about 6 to 8 minutes. Move the meat to low heat and continue cooking for about 4 minutes. Remove the meat from the grill slightly underdone; cool. Heat a sauce pot on the grill or side burner and add the olive oil, garlic, onion, beans, tomato sauce, cider vinegar, honey, brown sugar, and Tabasco. Bring to a boil, lower the heat, and simmer for 5 minutes. Slice the pork very thin, on an angle, and add to the bean mixture. Simmer for 15 minutes.

NUTRITIONAL INFORMATION

CALORIES 170

PROTEIN	14 g	CHOLESTEROL	26 mg
FAT	1.5 g	FIBER	7 g
SAT. FAT	0.5 g	SODIUM	420 mg

Substitute pork chops if veal chops are too costly.

VEAL CHOPS IN CACCAITORE SAUCE

Makes 4 servings
Temperature: grill high, then medium

4 shoulder veal chops or pork chops, well-trimmed
2 tablespoons olive oil
2 tablespoons balsamic vinegar
1 tablespoon fresh sage leaves, chopped
1/2 teaspoon Tabasco
fresh ground black pepper
2 cups Cacciatore Sauce (see page 86)

In a large bowl combine the olive oil, balsamic vinegar, sage leaves, Tabasco, and black pepper. Add the veal or pork chops and marinate for 2 hours in the refrigerator.

Preheat the grill.

Grill for 2 minutes on each side and remove. Place the chops in a sauce pan, add the cacciatore sauce, and simmer for 45 minutes.

NUTRITIONAL INFORMATION

CALORIES 370

PROTEIN	38 g	CHOLESTEROL	5 mg
FAT	19 g	FIBER	1 g
SAT. FAT	3.5 g	SODIUM	175 mg

Grilling the beef instead of pan-frying removes a lot of the fat. Having a few ounces of beef with all the vegetables is a great way to satisfy red meat cravings.

BEEF FAJITAS

Makes 6 servings
Temperature: grill high, then low

1¹/2 pounds flank steak

FOR THE MARINADE:
6 cloves Caramelized Garlic (see page 104)
1 teaspoon oregano
1 tablespoon paprika
1 tablespoon fresh cilantro, chopped
2 teaspoons cumin
1 teaspoon Tabasco
juice of 2 limes
2 tablespoons red wine vinegar
fresh ground black pepper

FOR THE FAJITAS:
3 red and green peppers, grilled
2 cups Caramelized Onions (see page 105)
2 large tomato wedges
fat free sour cream
salsa
6 flour tortillas, warmed

Marinate the flank steak overnight or for at least 2 hours in the refrigerator.

Preheat the grill to high. Remove the meat from the marinade and grill for 4 to 5 minutes on each side. Lower the heat and continue to cook the meat until desired doneness. Remove and allow the meat to sit for 5 minutes prior to slicing.

Preheat a heavy sauté or cast-iron pan. Slice the meat against the grain on an angle. Place the peppers, onions, and tomatoes in the pan and stir. Pour the meat juices into the pan, followed by the meat. Heat for a minute. Serve with warm flour tortillas and desired toppings.

NUTRITIONAL INFORMATION

CALORIES 240

PROTEIN	26 g	CHOLESTEROL	14 mg
FAT	9 g	FIBER	3 g
SAT. FAT	4 g	SODIUM	80 mg

Today most pork is very lean, making it a good low fat red meat alternative, although a leaner meat may produce a drier finished dish. This recipe saves the day when you donít have the time to watch over the grill or stove.

PORK CHOPS WITH
TOMATOES

Makes 4 servings
Temperature: medium to low grill or stovetop

4 lean boneless pork chops, about 1¹/2 pounds
2 tablespoons Pork Spice Blend (see page 163)
12 plum tomatoes, chopped
¹/4 cup Caramelized Onions (see page 105)
6 cloves Caramelized Garlic (see page 104)
4 tablespoons balsamic vinegar
¹/4 cup pitted green olives
1 tablespoon fresh basil, chopped
1 teaspoon Tabasco
fresh ground black pepper

Rub the chops with the Pork Spice Blend. Refrigerate for 2 hours.

Preheat a grill and a nonstick pan. Grill the chops for 2 minutes per side. Place in a skillet with the tomatoes, onions, garlic, vinegar, olives, basil, Tabasco, and black pepper. Simmer gently for 25 to 30 minutes.

NUTRITIONAL INFORMATION

CALORIES 300

PROTEIN	35 g	CHOLESTEROL	16 mg
FAT	10 g	FIBER	0 g
SAT. FAT	3.5 g	SODIUM	170 mg

SEAFOOD

I prefer to cook rope-cultured mussels because they're sweeter and more tender. Mussels should be alive when you're ready to cook them. Check by squeezing them and noticing if the shells are tightly closed. Next, scrub them under cold running water, removing the hairlike beard on the outside of the shells. Cook the mussels immediately.

CURRIED MUSSELS

Makes 4 servings
Temperature: high then low

4 pounds mussels, cleaned and debearded
1 tablespoon olive oil
¹/₄ cup onion, chopped
1 head Caramelized Garlic (see page 104)
1 tablespoon Madras curry
1 teaspoon hot pepper flakes
1 cup white wine or vegetable or chicken broth

Preheat a large stock or soup pot. Add the olive oil, onion, garlic, curry, and hot pepper flakes. Cook for 2 minutes. Add the mussels and wine or broth, cover and cook for 6 to 8 minutes or until the shells open. Shake the pot or stir every couple of minutes. Discard any mussels that do not open.

Remove the mussels from the shells and serve with the broth, or simply spoon mussels in their shells into large bowls and serve. Be sure to have a "shell dish" nearby.

NUTRITIONAL INFORMATION

CALORIES 210

PROTEIN	17 g	CHOLESTEROL	10 mg
FAT	7 g	FIBER	1 g
SAT. FAT	1.5 g	SODIUM	400 mg

The sea bass is a wonderful, neutral flavored fish that is complemented nicely with the pineapple.

SEA BASS & PINEAPPLE SKEWERS

Makes 4 servings
Temperature: grill high, then low; or 450°F oven, then 325°

1½ pounds sea bass, cut into 2 inch pieces
1 fresh pineapple, skinned, cored, and cut into 2-inch pieces
4 cloves Caramelized Garlic (see page 104)
1 tablespoon olive oil
2 tablespoons balsamic vinegar
1 tablespoon honey
½ teaspoon thyme
½ teaspoon rosemary
1 teaspoon paprika
pinch nutmeg
1 teaspoon Tabasco
fresh ground black pepper

Arrange the sea bass and the pineapple on skewers. Mix the garlic, olive oil, balsamic vinegar, honey, thyme, rosemary, paprika, nutmeg, Tabasco, and fresh ground black pepper. Pour over the skewers and marinate for 30 minutes.

Preheat the grill or oven. Grill for 2 to 3 minutes on each side on high. Baste with the marinade, then cook over a lower temperature for several minutes until done.

NUTRITIONAL INFORMATION

CALORIES 270

PROTEIN	36 g	CHOLESTEROL	18 mg
FAT	6 g	FIBER	2 g
SAT. FAT	1.5 g	SODIUM	95 mg

Salmon contains just the right amount of heart-healthy natural oils to keep it moist while cooking. Be careful not to overcook.

PEPPERED SALMON STEAKS

Makes 4 servings
Temperature: grill high then medium or 375°F oven

4 6- to 8-ounce salmon steaks
1 tablespoon prepared mustard
3 tablespoons coarsely crushed black peppercorns
¹/₄ teaspoon paprika
¹/₄ teaspoon garlic powder
1 teaspoon fresh thyme

Preheat the grill or oven. Coat the salmon steaks with the mustard. Mix the peppercorns, paprika, garlic powder, and fresh thyme. Coat the salmon steaks with the spice mixture. Cook on high heat for 2 minutes per side.

Cook for 2 to 3 additional minutes, or until done. The salmon will begin to flake slightly when done.

NUTRITIONAL INFORMATION

CALORIES 300

PROTEIN	33 g	CHOLESTEROL	0 mg
FAT	17 g	FIBER	0 g
SAT. FAT	4 g	SODIUM	140 mg

Monkfish is often called the "chicken of the sea." Its neutral taste and lobster-like texture makes it a much richer dish than chicken. For this recipe, you can substitute shrimp, scallops, or lobster for the monkfish if desired.

MONKFISH STIR-FRY (CHICKEN OF THE SEA)

Serves 4

Temperature: grill, wok, or sauté on medium, then low

1 1/2 pounds monkfish, cleaned
1 teaspoon olive oil
1 each red bell pepper, julienned
1 each green bell pepper, julienned
1/2 each pineapple, cut into wedges and grilled
3 each green onions or scallions, cut into 1-inch pieces
4 cloves Caramelized Garlic (see page 104)
1 tablespoon light soy sauce
1 teaspoon sesame oil
1 tablespoon ketchup
1 tablespoon honey

Preheat the grill. Brush the monkfish with the olive oil. Place the monkfish on the grill and cook for 2 minutes per side on medium heat. Remove; the fish will not be fully cooked. Cut the monkfish into silver dollar–size pieces. Sear the peppers, then set aside.

Preheat a wok or large sauté pan on the grill or side burner. Add the sesame oil, green onions or scallions, and garlic. Add the peppers, pineapple, soy sauce, ketchup, and honey. Add the monkfish and continue cooking until the fish is done.

NUTRITIONAL INFORMATION

CALORIES 210

PROTEIN	26 g	CHOLESTEROL	17 mg
FAT	4 g	FIBER	3 g
SAT. FAT	1 g	SODIUM	340 mg

Swordfish is available frozen in most food stores. Just ask the fish monger to cut a roast-size piece instead of the usual steak cut.

SWORDFISH ROAST

Makes 4 servings
Temperature: grill high-medium, then low

2¹/₂ pounds swordfish—one whole piece, not sliced
¹/₂ cup Fish Marinade (see page 161)
Cocktail Sauce (see page 84)

Marinate the swordfish for an hour in refrigerator. Preheat the grill. Place the swordfish on a high to medium grill, searing all sides. Then lower the temperature and cook slowly until fully cooked, about 25 minutes. Be careful not to overcook.

Remove and cool for 4 to 5 minutes. Slice into ¹/₂-inch slices.

Serve with the Cocktail Sauce (2 tablespoons per serving).

NUTRITIONAL INFORMATION

CALORIES 290

PROTEIN	40 g	CHOLESTEROL	11 mg
FAT	8 g	FIBER	0 g
SAT. FAT	2.5 g	SODIUM	390 mg

Serve warm on salad greens as an appetizer.

SHRIMP AND GARLIC SAUCE

Makes 4 servings
Temperature: grill high then medium, or 425°F oven then 350°

20 large shrimp, peeled and deveined (about 1 pound)
2 heads Caramelized Garlic (see page 104)
2 fresh lemons, juice only
¹/₄ cup balsamic vinegar
2 tablespoons olive oil
1 tablespoon fresh parsley, chopped
2 tablespoon fresh basil, chopped
3 each green onions or scallions, chopped
1 teaspoon Tabasco sauce
fresh ground black pepper

Place the shrimp on a skewer. Remove the garlic cloves from the heads and place in a nonreactive bowl. Add the lemon juice, balsamic vinegar, olive oil, parsley, basil, green onions or scallions, Tabasco, and fresh ground black pepper. Mix all the ingredients and pour over the skewered shrimp. Marinate in the refrigerator for 30 minutes.

Preheat the grill or oven. Place the skewered shrimp on the grill on high heat or on an ovenproof platter in the oven for 2 minutes on each side. Move to medium heat and grill or bake for an additional 4 to 5 minutes, or until done. Brush the shrimp with the garlic sauce.

Serve with salad greens, over rice, or with pasta.

NUTRITIONAL INFORMATION

CALORIES 120

PROTEIN	15 g	CHOLESTEROL	135 mg
FAT	4 g	FIBER	0 g
SAT. FAT	0.5 g	SODIUM	160 mg

The mild taste of spinach goes very well with the delicate taste of flounder. Flounder cooks very quickly, so use caution or the fillet will fall apart.

STUFFED FLOUNDER WITH SPINACH

Makes 4 servings
Temperature: grill medium or 375°F oven

8 pieces flounder fillet, about 2 pounds
1 cup frozen spinach, thawed and drained
1/4 cup feta cheese
6 cloves Caramelized Garlic (see page 104)
1/4 cup reduced-fat mayonnaise
4 tablespoons bread crumbs
juice from 2 lemons
1 teaspoon dried oregano
1 teaspoon paprika
2 tablespoons olive oil
low fat vegetable spray
1 teaspoons hot sauce
fresh ground black pepper

Preheat the grill or oven. Lightly grease a nonstick pan with low fat vegetable spray. In a medium bowl combine the feta cheese, garlic, mayonnaise, juice from one lemon, oregano, and hot sauce. Add the spinach and bread crumbs and mix well.

Lay the flounder fillets on a flat surface. Place an equal amount of the filling at the middle of each fillet, then fold the bottom and top ends over the stuffing. Place the fish, seam side down, into the greased pan. Leave a small space between each piece of fish.

Drizzle the remaining olive oil, lemon juice, paprika, and fresh ground black pepper on top of the stuffed fillets.

Bake on the grill or oven for 8 to 10 minutes, or until the flounder becomes milky white and begins to flake.

NUTRITIONAL INFORMATION

CALORIES 380

PROTEIN	47 g	CHOLESTEROL	14 mg
FAT	15 g	FIBER	2 g
SAT. FAT	3.5 g	SODIUM	460 mg

A flour tortilla is a good staple to have in the refrigerator. Tortillas can be used for quesadillas, burritos, tacos, and, while on the run, a quick rollup sandwich. You can make this recipe wthout heating up the grill. Or, you can get very fancy by using seared rub chicken, pulled pork, BBQ beef, or smoked seafood. Go ahead—get crazy!

SHRIMP ROLLUPS

Makes 4

4 8- to 10-inch flour tortillas
1/2 pound small precooked cocktail shrimp
8 lettuce leaves
1/2 cup alfalfa sprouts
1/4 cup shredded carrots
1/4 cup cooked corn
1/4 cup canned black beans, rinsed
4 tablespoons lite salad dressing—tomato vinaigrette, or your favorite flavor

Assemble one tortilla at a time. Lay each tortilla flat and place one-quarter of the lettuce, sprouts, carrots, shrimp, corn, beans, and dressing in the center. Fold the tortilla, then roll up tightly. Serve immediately or wrap in plastic to keep from drying out.

NUTRITIONAL INFORMATION

CALORIES 230

PROTEIN	15 g	CHOLESTEROL	34 mg
FAT	4 g	FIBER	2 g
SAT. FAT	0.5 g	SODIUM	560 mg

POULTRY

Cooking the chicken with the skin on will result in a finished dish that is moist and flavorful. Remove the skin after the chicken is cooked, prior to eating. No orange juice in the house? Any citrus juice will complement this chicken dish.

ORANGE CHICKEN

Makes 4 servings
Temperature: grill medium, then low, or 350°F oven

1 whole chicken, cut into 12 pieces (about 3 pounds)
2 cups orange juice
1 tablespoon light soy sauce
1 orange, cut into 8 pieces
1 teaspoon sesame oil
2 tablespoons fresh ginger, peeled, cut into strips
1 head Caramelized Garlic (see page 104)
1 teaspoon hot pepper flakes

Marinate the chicken pieces in orange juice and soy sauce overnight in the refrigerator. Remove the chicken from the marinade. Discard the marinade.

Preheat the grill or oven. Place the chicken on a medium temperature grill and cook 8 to 10 minutes until lightly brown, then lower the heat and cook until done. Place the orange pieces on the grill, skin side down. Allow to lightly char on the outside.

Preheat a sauté pan on the side burner or grill. Add the sesame oil, garlic, and ginger. Cook 30 seconds, then add the orange pieces, cooked chicken, and hot pepper flakes. Toss for 2 minutes and serve.

NUTRITIONAL INFORMATION

CALORIES 240

PROTEIN	37 g	CHOLESTEROL	6 mg
FAT	6 g	FIBER	0 g
SAT. FAT	1.5 g	SODIUM	240 mg

Once you start eating turkey burgers, you'll never want another drive-thru burger again!

ULTIMATE TURKEY BURGER

Makes 6 to 8 burgers
Temperature: grill high-medium

2 pounds ground turkey, 93% fat free
$^1/_4$ cup finely chopped onion
2 tablespoons mustard
6 cloves Caramelized Garlic (see page 104)
4 tablespoons steak sauce
$^1/_4$ cup finely chopped mushrooms
2 each jalapeño peppers, grilled, seeded, and chopped
1 tablespoon chopped fresh cilantro
fresh ground black pepper

In a medium bowl, combine all of the ingredients and mix with a fork, taking care not to overwork the meat. Divide the mixture into 6 to 8 equal portions and form into patties. Cover and refrigerate for 2 hours.

Preheat the grill. Place the burgers on a hot grill for 2 minutes on each side. Lower the heat to medium, and cook for 7 to 8 minutes or until done.

NUTRITIONAL INFORMATION

CALORIES 160			
PROTEIN	28 g	CHOLESTEROL	4 mg
FAT	3.5 g	FIBER	0 g
SAT. FAT	0.5 g	SODIUM	150 mg

Kebobs that are prepared ahead of time make an ideal dinner party entree. Just light the grill and cook!

SWEET AND SOUR TURKEY KEBOBS

Makes 4 servings
Temperature: grill high, then low

2-pound skinless turkey breast, cut into 1-inch cubes
1/2 fresh pineapple, skinned, cored, and cut into wedges
2 red bell peppers, cut into 1-inch squares
1 cup orange juice
1/4 cup cider vinegar
2 tablespoons honey
2 tablespoons brown sugar
2 tablespoons ketchup
1 tablespoon lite soy sauce
1 teaspoon Tabasco

Arrange the turkey, pineapple, and peppers on skewers. In a medium bowl combine the orange juice, cider vinegar, honey, brown sugar, ketchup, soy sauce, and Tabasco. Pour over the turkey kebobs and marinate in the refrigerator for 2 hours.

Preheat the grill.

Place the turkey kebobs on a hot grill and grill for 4 to 5 minutes on each side, basting the kebobs with the marinade. Move to a low heat and continue cooking until done.

NUTRITIONAL INFORMATION

CALORIES 270			
PROTEIN	41 g	CHOLESTEROL	24 mg
FAT	1.5 g	FIBER	2 g
SAT. FAT	0 g	SODIUM	320 mg

This recipe is in honor of all the great folks at the Asparagus Festival in Stockton, California, where several tons of the sweet spears are served in three days!

GRILLED CHICKEN CUTLETS WITH ASPARAGUS

Makes 4 servings
Temperature: grill high then low

4 6-ounce chicken cutlets, pounded lightly
1/2 pound or 12 asparagus spears, blanched al dente
3 tablespoons olive oil
6 cloves Caramelized Garlic (see page 104)
1 lemon, zest and juice
1/4 cup white wine
1 tablespoon fresh chopped sage leaves
fresh ground black pepper

Use 2 tablespoons of olive oil to brush the asparagus bundles and then the chicken breasts. Preheat the grill. Place the chicken on high heat, sear and then turn after a minute or when the chicken is lightly brown.

Grill the asparagus on high heat until hot.

Preheat a sauté pan on the grill or side burner. Add the remaining tablespoon of olive oil, then add the chicken, garlic, lemon zest and juice, white wine, sage, and black pepper. Cook for 2 to 3 minutes, then place the asparagus on top. Cover the sauté pan on a side burner or close the cover of the grill for 4 minutes, then serve.

NUTRITIONAL INFORMATION

CALORIES 270

PROTEIN	41 g	CHOLESTEROL	4 mg
FAT	9 g	FIBER	4 g
SAT. FAT	1.5 g	SODIUM	130 mg

If you do not have a rotisserie on your grill, try this easy setup with a soda or beer can. Leave some liquid inside the can to steam the inside of the bird while the outside roasts.

CHICKEN ON A CAN

Makes 4 servings
Temperature: grill medium on indirect heat

1 soda or beer can, opened, with $^1/3$ of the beverage left in the can
1 3-pound chicken, whole
8 cloves Caramelized Garlic (see page 104)
1 tablespoon dried rosemary
1 teaspoon dried thyme
fresh ground black pepper

Rub the outside of the chicken with garlic, rosemary, thyme, and black pepper.

Preheat the grill. Place the opening in the chicken over the top of a soda or beer can, then position the "canned" chicken on a medium grill, on an indirect heat. Close the cover of the grill. Cook for 1$^1/2$ hours, turning the chicken every 20 minutes. Remove the chicken when the internal temperature reaches 160°F with an instant-read or meat thermometer.

Allow to cool 10 minutes before removing from the can.

NOTE: Use your favorite beer or soda to flavor the chicken. A lemon soda gives a slight lemon flavor, cola a caramel flavor, etc.

NUTRITIONAL INFORMATION

CALORIES 200			
PROTEIN	35 g	CHOLESTEROL	115 mg
FAT	5 g	FIBER	0 g
SAT. FAT	1.5 g	SODIUM	125 mg

This is not just another burger—it's a Paella Burger! Save on the food budget so you can splurge on some new clothes.

TURKEY BURGER WITH PAELLA RICE

Makes 6 servings
Temperature: grill high, then medium

1¹/2 pounds ground turkey, very cold
2 tablespoons barbecue sauce
¹/4 medium onion, chopped fine
6 cloves Caramelized Garlic (see page 104)
1 teaspoon ground cumin
1 tablespoon cilantro, chopped
¹/2 teaspoon hot sauce
Paella Rice (see page 102)

In a medium bowl, combine all the ingredients and mix with a fork, taking care not to overwork the meat. Divide the mixture into 4 to 6 equal portions and form into hamburger patties.

Chill for 2 hours.

Preheat the grill. Place the burgers on the grill over high heat and cook until no longer pink in the center. Remove and finish cooking in paella rice for 5 minutes.

NUTRITIONAL INFORMATION

CALORIES 330

PROTEIN	32 g	CHOLESTEROL	32 mg
FAT	6 g	FIBER	2 g
SAT. FAT	1 g	SODIUM	370 mg

Cutting the chicken into finger-size pieces allows the meat to absorb additional flavor. This is a favorite recipe for kids of all ages!

GARLIC & ROSEMARY CHICKEN FINGERS

Serves 6
Temperature: grill high/medium

2 pounds chicken cutlets, cut into 1-inch strips
2 tablespoons olive oil
1 head Caramelized Garlic (see page 104)
1 tablespoon rosemary, crushed
1 teaspoon hot sauce
fresh ground black pepper

Marinate the chicken strips in the olive oil, garlic, rosemary, hot sauce, and black pepper for 2 hours in the refrigerator.

Preheat the grill to high.

Place the chicken on the grill and cook for 2 to 3 minutes per side. Serve with your favorite dipping sauce.

NUTRITIONAL INFORMATION

CALORIES 210

PROTEIN	31 g	CHOLESTEROL	2 mg
FAT	8 g	FIBER	0 g
SAT. FAT	1.5 g	SODIUM	80 mg

Once all the ingredients have been assembled and cut, the cooking time of this dish is very quick.

BROCCOLI & CHICKEN

Serves 4
Temperature: high then medium

1 pound boneless chicken breasts, cut into very thin strips
2 cups broccoli, cut into florets
2 green onions, chopped
4 cloves Caramelized Garlic (see page 104)
1 red bell pepper, thinly sliced
1 teaspoon sesame oil
1 tablespoon lite soy sauce
1 tablespoon hoisin sauce
1/4 cup chicken broth

Preheat a wok or sauté pan. Add the sesame oil and chicken and stir fry until the chicken turns a light color. Add the broccoli, green onions, garlic, bell pepper, soy sauce, hoisin, and broth. Cook for 2 to 3 minutes.

NUTRITIONAL INFORMATION

CALORIES 170			
PROTEIN	25 g	CHOLESTEROL	7 mg
FAT	4 g	FIBER	2 g
SAT. FAT	1 g	SODIUM	160 mg

Be creative! Add asparagus, mushrooms, or any other favorite vegetable to the chicken. The chicken and peppers can be served warm on top of fresh spinach, arugula, or other salad greens.

CHICKEN WITH ROAST
PEPPERS

Makes 4 servings
Temperature: grill high then medium

4 6-ounce boneless chicken breasts, cleaned and lightly pounded
2 red, yellow, or green bell peppers, cut in half and deseeded
1 tablespoon olive oil
6 cloves Caramelized Garlic, crushed (see page 104)
1 lime, juice only
1 teaspoon dried basil
1 teaspoon Tabasco
fresh ground black pepper
1/2 cup Mango Relish (see page 88)

Preheat the grill. Brush the chicken breasts with the olive oil and lime juice. Add the crushed caramelized garlic, basil, Tabasco, and black pepper. Place the chicken and peppers on a very hot grill and sear on both sides for 2 to 3 minutes. Move the chicken to a medium heat and cook approximately 5 to 6 minutes. Remove the peppers when they are seared and place in a bowl. Cover to allow steam to loosen their skins. Peel the pepper skins, then cut the peppers into strips.

Remove the chicken breasts from the grill. Thinly slice the breasts on an angle. Add the peppers to the sliced chicken. Top with mango relish.

NUTRITIONAL INFORMATION

CALORIES 280

PROTEIN	36 g	CHOLESTEROL	19 mg
FAT	7 g	FIBER	2 g
SAT. FAT	1.5 g	SODIUM	85 mg

Tired of the same ol' chicken? Try this version, without the usual barbecue-style sauce. Omit the margarine from the candy glaze, and its a nonfat sauce!

CANDIED CHICKEN

Makes 8 servings
Temperature: grill medium, then low

2 whole chickens, cut into small pieces, or 4 6-ounce skinless breasts
1 cup Poultry Spice Blend (see page 164)

CANDY GLAZE:
1/2 cup crushed pecans
1/2 cup brown sugar
1 cup cane syrup
1 cup orange juice
8 cloves Caramelized Garlic (see page 104)
1 teaspoon dried thyme
1 tablespoon margerine
pinch nutmeg

Rub the chickens with the Poultry Spice Blend and refrigerate for an hour.

Preheat the grill. Place the chicken on medium heat and cook for 5 to 10 minutes, until it begins to color. Move to a low or indirect heat and slowly cook for 45 minutes to 1 hour, until the juices run clear. Baste with Candy Glaze during the last 10 minutes.

FOR GLAZE: Preheat the grill or side burner. In a small nonreactive saucepan, combine all the ingredients and simmer for 5 minutes. Brush the glaze on the chicken during the last 10 minutes of cooking.

NUTRITIONAL INFORMATION

CALORIES 250

PROTEIN	3 g	CHOLESTEROL	55 mg
FAT	3 g	FIBER	5 g
SAT. FAT	0.5 g	SODIUM	55 mg

SPICE RUBS & MARINADES

Use this vinaigrette as a marinade for vegetables, meats, or seafood and as a basic vinaigrette for salad greens.

GRILLING VINAIGRETTE

Makes about 1 cup

$^1/_2$ cup tomato or vegetable juice
$^1/_4$ cup balsamic vinegar
1 tablespoon olive oil
1 tablespoon horseradish
2 tablespoons pitted green olives, chopped
4 cloves Caramelized Garlic (see page 104)
1 green onion, chopped
1 teaspoon dry mustard
1 teaspoon dried basil
1 teaspoon Tabasco
fresh ground black pepper

Combine all the ingredients until well blended. Cover and allow the vinaigrette to sit at room temperature for 2 to 3 hours.

Use this as a marinade for vegetables, meats, or seafood and as a basic vinai-grette for salad greens.

GRILLING MARINADE

Makes about 1 cup

1/2 cup apple juice
1/4 cup cider vinegar
juice of 1 lime
1 tablespoon olive oil
1 tablespoon dijon mustard
1 tablespoon ketchup
4 cloves Caramelized Garlic (see page 104)
1 green onion, chopped
1 teaspoon paprika
1 teaspoon thyme
1 teaspoon Tabasco
fresh ground black pepper

Combine all the ingredients until well blended. Cover and allow the marinade to sit at room temperature for 2 to 3 hours.

NUTRITIONAL INFORMATION
(PER 2 TABLESPOONS)

CALORIES 35			
PROTEIN	0 g	CHOLESTEROL	4 mg
FAT	2 g	FIBER	0 g
SAT. FAT	0 g	SODIUM	70 mg

A fish marinade should be highly seasoned because it's used for 30 minutes or less.

FISH MARINADE

Makes about 1 cup

juice of 2 lemons
juice of 2 limes
1 tablespoon olive oil
1 tablespoon dijon mustard
1 tablespoon honey
4 cloves Caramelized Garlic (see page 104)
1 green onion, chopped
1 teaspoon paprika
1 teaspoon thyme
1 teaspoon basil
1 teaspoon Tabasco
fresh ground black pepper

Combine all the ingredients until well blended. Cover and allow the marinade to sit at room temperature for 2 to 3 hours.

NUTRITIONAL INFORMATION
(PER 2 TABLESPOONS)

CALORIES 33			
PROTEIN	0 g	CHOLESTEROL	5 mg
FAT	2 g	FIBER	0 g
SAT. FAT	0 g	SODIUM	50 mg

Marinades are the best way to keep foods moist while flavoring them at the same time.

PORK TENDERLOIN MARINADE

Makes about 1¹/₄ cups

1 cup orange juice
juice of 2 limes
8 cloves Caramelized Garlic (see page 104)
1 tablespoon lite soy sauce
1 teaspoon curry powder
1 teaspoon ground cumin

Combine all the ingredients in a small bowl and mix well.

NUTRITIONAL INFORMATION
(PER 2 TABLESPOONS)

CALORIES 25

PROTEIN	1 g	CHOLESTEROL	0 mg
FAT	0 g	FIBER	0 g
SAT. FAT	0 g	SODIUM	70 mg

PORK SPICE BLEND

Makes 7 tablespoons

1 tablespoon garlic powder
2 tablespoons paprika
1 tablespoon dried thyme leaves
1 tablespoon dried rosemary
1 tablespoon ground cumin
1 teaspoon cayenne pepper
1 teaspoon fresh ground black pepper

Combine all the ingredients and mix well. Store in a tightly sealed container until ready to use.

NUTRITIONAL INFORMATION
(PER TABLESPOON)

CALORIES 15			
PROTEIN	1 g	CHOLESTEROL	3 mg
FAT	0.5 g	FIBER	1 g
SAT. FAT	0 g	SODIUM	0 mg

POULTRY SPICE BLEND

Makes 7 tablespoons

1 tablespoon garlic powder
2 tablespoons paprika
1 tablespoon dried thyme
1 tablespoon dried rosemary
1 tablespoon dried ground sage
1 teaspoon dry mustard
1/2 teaspoon nutmeg
1/2 teaspoon cayenne
1 teaspoon fresh ground black pepper

Combine all the ingredients and mix well. Store in a tightly sealed container until ready to use.

NUTRITIONAL INFORMATION
(PER TABLESPOON)

CALORIES 15			
PROTEIN	1 g	CHOLESTEROL	3 mg
FAT	0.5 g	FIBER	1 g
SAT. FAT	0 g	SODIUM	0 mg

BEEF SPICE BLEND

Makes ¹/2 cup

1 tablespoon garlic powder
3 tablespoons paprika
1 tablespoon dried thyme leaves
1 tablespoon dried rosemary
1 tablespoon ground basil
¹/2 tablespoon oregano
1 teaspoon cayenne pepper
1 teaspoon fresh ground black pepper

Combine all the ingredients and mix well. Store in a tightly sealed container until ready to use.

NUTRITIONAL INFORMATION
(PER TABLESPOON)

CALORIES 15			
PROTEIN	1 g	CHOLESTEROL	3 mg
FAT	0.5 g	FIBER	1 g
SAT. FAT	0 g	SODIUM	0 mg

SEAFOOD SPICE BLEND

Makes 3 tablespoons

1 teaspoon garlic powder
1 tablespoon paprika
$1/2$ tablespoon dried thyme leaves
$1/2$ tablespoon dried rosemary
1 teaspoon dried parsley
1 teaspoon fresh ground black pepper

Combine all the ingredients and mix well. Store in a tightly sealed container until ready to use.

NUTRITIONAL INFORMATION
(PER TABLESPOON)

CALORIES 15

PROTEIN	1 g	CHOLESTEROL	3 mg
FAT	0 g	FIBER	1 g
SAT. FAT	0 g	SODIUM	0 mg

SOUTHWEST SPICE BLEND

Makes ¹/₄ cup

1 teaspoon garlic powder
1 tablespoon paprika
¹/₂ tablespoon dried thyme leaves
1 tablespoon ground cumin
¹/₂ tablespoon ground coriander
1 teaspoon dried cilantro
¹/₂ teaspoon cayenne
1 teaspoon fresh ground black pepper

Combine all the ingredients and mix well. Store in a tightly sealed container until ready to use.

NUTRITIONAL INFORMATION
(PER TABLESPOON)

CALORIES 15			
PROTEIN	1 g	CHOLESTEROL	3 mg
FAT	0 g	FIBER	1 g
SAT. FAT	0 g	SODIUM	0 mg

The traditional ingredient in pesto is basil, although you can use other fragrant leaves as a nice taste alternative (see substitutions below).

PESTO

Makes about 1 cup

1 cup packed fresh basil leaves, washed and dried—handle gently!
1 head Caramelized Garlic (see page 104)
2 tablespoons walnuts, chopped
3 tablespoons grated parmesan cheese
3 tablespoons olive oil

Place the garlic and walnuts in a food processor or blender. Puree gently. Add the basil and slightly grind. Do not grind too long or you will actually be cooking the tender leaves. Add the olive oil and cheese and process until it makes a paste. Refrigerate until ready to use.

SUBSTITIONS:

cilantro pesto: use $^1/_2$ cup plus 2 tomatillos or green tomatoes
mint pesto: use $^1/_3$ cup plus $^2/_3$ cup fresh spinach
sage pesto: use two tablespoons plus $^1/_4$ cup fresh parsley

NUTRITIONAL INFORMATION
(PER 2 TABLESPOONS)

CALORIES 35			
PROTEIN	1 g	CHOLESTEROL	1 mg
FAT	3.5 g	FIBER	0 g
SAT. FAT	0.5 g	SODIUM	20 mg

BEVERAGES

Here is a drink for a celebration—or for just sleeping in on the weekend!

MIMOSAS

Makes 2 drinks

1 cup diet lemon soda
1/2 cup mango, papaya, passion fruit, or orange juice
2 scoops lemon sorbet (1/2 cup total)
4 tablespoons cranberry juice
2 sprigs fresh mint

In two champagne or margarita glasses, divide the fruit juice and lemon soda. Place one scoop of sorbet in each glass. Top with the cranberry juice and mint. Serve immediately.

NUTRITIONAL INFORMATION

CALORIES 120

PROTEIN	0 g	CHOLESTEROL	31 mg
FAT	0 g	FIBER	0 g
SAT. FAT	0 g	SODIUM	25 mg

This smoothie is an excellent beverage to drink an hour before a workout or right after. You may even want to serve it as a dessert.

BANANA SMOOTHIE

Makes 2 servings

1 cup frozen sliced bananas
1 tablespoon low fat peanut butter
$^1/_2$ cup fat free milk
$^1/_2$ cup plain low fat yogurt
$^1/_2$ cup crushed ice

Place the bananas in a blender and puree. Add the peanut butter, fat free milk, yogurt, and ice. Blend until smooth.

NUTRITIONAL INFORMATION

CALORIES 170

PROTEIN	8 g	CHOLESTEROL	27 mg
FAT	4 g	FIBER	2 g
SAT. FAT	1.5 g	SODIUM	120 mg

Serve with a spoon or a straw—either way, this drink will cool you off!

BERRY SMOOTHIE

Makes 2 servings

1 cup frozen unsweetened strawberries, blueberries, raspberries, or blackberries
juice from $^1/_2$ lemon
1 cup frozen low fat vanilla yogurt
$^1/_2$ cup fat free milk

Place the berries in a blender and puree. Add the lemon juice, frozen yogurt, and milk. Blend until smooth.

NUTRITIONAL INFORMATION

CALORIES 160

PROTEIN	4 g	CHOLESTEROL	31 mg
FAT	1.5 g	FIBER	2 g
SAT. FAT	1 g	SODIUM	90 mg

This smoothie will almost taste like biting into an apple pie!

APPLE SMOOTHIE

Makes 2 servings

1 cup macintosh apple, sliced, peeled, and soaked in juice of 1/2 lemon
1 cup apple juice, frozen
1 cup plain low fat yogurt
1/2 cup crushed ice
pinch of cinnamon

Freeze an apple juice box or a cup of apple juice. Place the apples in a blender with the lemon juice and puree. Add the frozen apple juice, yogurt, crushed ice, and cinnamon. Blend until smooth.

NUTRITIONAL INFORMATION

CALORIES 170			
PROTEIN	7 g	CHOLESTEROL	34 mg
FAT	2 g	FIBER	1 g
SAT. FAT	1.5 g	SODIUM	90 mg

Once you get beyond the fact that this drink contains carrots, you'll want seconds.

CARROT APPLE JUICE

Makes 2 1-cup servings

1 carrot, scrubbed well and chopped
1 unpeeled apple, washed and chopped
juice of $^1/_2$ lemon
$^1/_2$ rib celery, washed and chopped
1 cup crushed ice
2 tablespoons reduced fat peanut butter
$^1/_2$ cup apple juice

In a juicer or blender, add the carrot, apple, celery, and lemon juice and blend. Add the crushed ice, peanut butter, and apple juice. Mix until combined.

NUTRITIONAL INFORMATION

CALORIES 170

PROTEIN	5 g	CHOLESTEROL	29 mg
FAT	6 g	FIBER	4 g
SAT. FAT	1 g	SODIUM	110 mg

I get a kick out of this drink, especially with the jalapeño.

TOMATO JALAPEÑO LIME JUICE

Makes 2 1-cup servings

1¹/₂ cups tomato juice, chilled
¹/₂ cup crushed ice
1 jalapeño, seeded and chopped
juice of 1 lime

Place the ice in a blender. Add the jalapeño and blend. Add the tomato juice and lime juice. Blend until combined.

NUTRITIONAL INFORMATION

CALORIES 45

PROTEIN	2 g	CHOLESTEROL	13 mg
FAT	0 g	FIBER	1 g
SAT. FAT	0 g	SODIUM	660 mg

Punch is usually associated with celebrations. This refreshing beverage will also quench your thirst.

A STRIKING PUNCH

Makes over 3 pints

juice of 4 limes
juice of 4 lemons
juice of 4 oranges
12 ounces papaya juice
12 ounces cranberry juice
12 ounces sugar-free lemon soda

Mix all the ingredients except the lemon soda and chill for an hour. Add the lemon soda and serve with fresh mint and lime slices.

NUTRITIONAL INFORMATION

CALORIES 90			
PROTEIN	1 g	CHOLESTEROL	24 mg
FAT	0 g	FIBER	2 g
SAT. FAT	0 g	SODIUM	15 mg

DESSERTS

Find time in your hectic day to make these reduced fat cookies with regular sugar instead of a substitute. You'll burn off the extra calories. Splurge with a couple, and you'll feel as if you've had your cake and eaten it, too!

OATMEAL COOKIES

Makes one and 1 1/2 to 2 dozen cookies
Temperature: 350°F oven

6 tablespoons margarine
1/4 cup applesauce
1/2 cup brown sugar
1/2 cup sugar
1/4 cup egg substitute, or 2 egg whites
1 1/2 cups rolled oats (not quick-cooking)
3/4 cup flour
1/4 teaspoon salt
1/2 teaspoon baking soda
1/4 cup raisins
1 teaspoon vanilla
2 tablespoons pecans, chopped

Preheat the oven.

Mix the margarine, applesauce, brown sugar, sugar, egg, and vanilla. Beat until creamy. Sift the flour with salt and baking soda. Add to the creamed mixture, blending well. Fold in the oats, raisins, and nuts.

Make into 1-inch balls and place on a cookie sheet. Bake for 9 to 11 minutes, or until the edges begin to set. *Do not overbake!* The cookies will carry the heat and continue to bake when removed from the oven.

NOTE: For Chocolate Oatmeal Cookies, sift 2 tablespoons cocoa powder with the flour.

NUTRITIONAL INFORMATION

CALORIES 100

PROTEIN	2 g	CHOLESTEROL	17 mg
FAT	3.5 g	FIBER	1 g
SAT. FAT	0.5 g	SODIUM	100 mg

Bananas are the world's most perfect food. I always have extra around, and there are always a few extra ripe ones. Peel and chop the ripe bananas, pack in a plastic bag, and freeze until you need them.

BANANA NUT MUFFINS

Makes 10 to 12
Temperature: 350°F oven

1/4 cup plus 2 tablespoons molasses
3 tablespoons honey
1/4 cup egg substitute or 2 egg whites, beaten
1/4 cup margarine
1/4 cup applesauce
1 cup mashed ripe bananas
1/2 cup raisins
1/4 cup walnuts, chopped
1 cup whole wheat flour
1/2 cup rolled oats (not quick-cooking)
1/2 teaspoon baking powder
1 teaspoon baking soda
1 teaspoon cinnamon
1/4 teaspoon allspice
pinch nutmeg and ginger

Grease a nonstick muffin pan with vegetable spray or use muffin liners. Preheat the oven.

Beat the margarine with the eggs and add the applesauce. Mix the molasses and honey. Warm slightly, allow to cool, then add to the margarine and applesauce. Stir.

Add the bananas, nuts, and raisins. Fold in the flour, oats, baking powder, baking soda, cinnamon, allspice, nutmeg, and ginger.

Place the batter in the muffin pans filling each slot to three quarters full. Bake for 18 to 20 minutes.

NOTE: For Banana Quick Bread, bake in a loaf pan for 45 to 50 minutes.

NUTRITIONAL INFORMATION

CALORIES 150			
PROTEIN	2 g	CHOLESTEROL	24 mg
FAT	6 g	FIBER	1 g
SAT. FAT	1 g	SODIUM	180 mg

Most carrot bread and muffins I have tasted are usually too sweet and contain a lot of fat. Try this naturally sweet and low fat version, and you'll never go back to the other types. Slice the carrot bread when cool and wrap in plastic wrap for a good midday snack on the run.

CARROT NUT BREAD

Makes one loaf, 12 slices
Temperature: 350°F oven

1/4 cup skim milk
1/2 cup corn syrup
2 tablespoons honey
1/4 cup egg substitute or 2 egg whites, beaten
1/4 cup margerine
1/4 cup applesauce
1/2 cup shredded carrots
1/2 cup shredded zucchini
1/2 cup raisins
1/4 cup walnuts, chopped
1 cup whole wheat flour
1/2 cup rolled oats (not quick-cooking)
1/2 teaspoon baking powder
1 teaspoon baking soda
1 teaspoon cinnamon
1/4 teaspoon allspice
pinch nutmeg

Grease a nonstick loaf pan with vegetable spray. Preheat the oven.

Beat the margarine with the eggs and add the applesauce. Mix the corn syrup and honey. Warm slightly, allow to cool, then add to the margarine and applesauce.

Add the milk, carrots, zucchini, nuts, and raisins. Fold in the flour, oats, baking powder, cinnamon, allspice, nutmeg, and baking soda.

Pour the batter into the loaf pan and bake for 45 to 50 minutes, or until a toothpick or skewer comes out clean.

NUTRITIONAL INFORMATION

CALORIES 180

PROTEIN	4 g	CHOLESTEROL	30 mg
FAT	6 g	FIBER	2 g
SAT. FAT	1 g	SODIUM	210 mg

Do not sweat making this dessert. Chefs are able to make crepes by the dozen very quickly because they make them over and over. The first couple you attempt may be too thick or break apart, but you will be making crepes by the dozen in no time.

FRUIT CREPES

Makes 8 to 10 crepes
Temperature: medium

1/2 cup whole wheat flour
2 tablespoons almonds, crushed
1 ounce egg substitute (2 tablespoons)
1/3 cup fat free milk
1 teaspoon vanilla
1 teaspoon lemon zest
vegetable cooking spray

Place the flour in a bowl and make a well. Add the almonds and egg substitute, then slowly add the milk while whisking smooth. Mix in the vanilla and lemon zest. Do not overmix. Cover the batter and allow to rest for 30 minutes.

Spray a nonstick 8-inch egg pan with vegetable spray and preheat. Spoon a couple of tablespoons of batter in the bottom, just enough to lightly coat the bottom by tilting the pan. Cook for a minute or until the edges set. Flip, then continue to cook for 1 to 2 minutes until fully cooked. Remove the cooked crepe and repeat the process.

Crepes can be stacked one on top of the other after they are cool.

Roll crepes with assorted summer fruit fillings such as sliced peaches or berries, and top with frozen yogurt.

NUTRITIONAL INFORMATION

CALORIES 35

PROTEIN	2 g	CHOLESTEROL	5 mg
FAT	5 g	FIBER	1 g
SAT. FAT	0 g	SODIUM	10 mg

Grapefruit is very refreshing, packed with fiber, and low in calories. The granola and honey provide a wonderfully sweet crunch. Add a glass of skim milk for a low fat breakfast.

GRAPEFRUIT CRUNCH

Makes 2 servings
Temperature: grill medium or 350°F oven

2 large grapefruit, peeled and segmented
2 tablespoons honey
1/2 cup Granola (see page 187)
3 low fat graham crackers
vegetable spray

Spray a small oven casserole with the vegetable spray. Line the bottom of the pan with graham crackers. Place the grapefruit segments on top. Cover with the granola and honey. Bake for 4 to 5 minutes and serve.

NUTRITIONAL INFORMATION

CALORIES 300

PROTEIN	4 g	CHOLESTEROL	68 mg
FAT	3.5 g	FIBER	5 g
SAT. FAT	0.5 g	SODIUM	115 mg

Baking with unsweetened cocoa powder instead of chocolate is a healthy way to get your chocolate fix. There is no harm in treating yourself. The combination of chocolate and baked apple is a pleasing taste treat in this dessert.

BAKED CHOCOLATE APPLES

Makes 4 servings
Temperature: medium grill or 350°F oven

4 medium Rome or baking apples
^{1}/2 cup apple juice
4 tablespoons reduced fat cream cheese
1 tablespoon unsweetened cocoa powder
2 tablespoons honey
1 teaspoon cinnamon
pinch nutmeg

Preheat the oven or grill. Cut the stem end of the apples approximately 2 inches around and 1-inch deep, on an angle. Save the tops to place back on after filling the apples. Core the apples ^{3}/4 through—do not core completely through the bottom.

Mix the cream cheese, honey, and cocoa powder. Fill the inside of the apples with the cream cheese mix. Place the stem back on top of the apples.

Put the apples in a small baking dish. Mix the cinnamon and nutmeg into the apple juice. Cover the apples with the juice and bake for 5 to 7 minutes. Uncover for 5 additional minutes. The apples are done when you can slide a knife easily through the flesh.

NUTRITIONAL INFORMATION

CALORIES 140

PROTEIN	2 g	CHOLESTEROL	33 mg
FAT	2 g	FIBER	4 g
SAT. FAT	1 g	SODIUM	55 mg

Several years ago, it was hard to find good tortillas. Today, however, tortillas are readily available, and your imagination can provide infinite possibilities for filling them.

CARAMELIZED PEAR BURRITO

Makes 4 servings
Temperature: medium

4 ripe pears, cored and chopped
4 8- to 10-inch flour tortillas
1 tablespoon brown sugar
1 tablespoon dark corn syrup or honey
vegetable spray
4 tablespoons plain low fat yogurt
1 teaspoon cinnamon
1/2 teaspoon nutmeg

Spray a nonstick sauté pan with vegetable spray and preheat.
   Add the chopped pears, brown sugar, and honey. Cook until light brown. Cool slightly, then add the yogurt, cinnamon, and nutmeg.
   Place the pear filling inside warm flour tortillas and wrap.

NUTRITIONAL INFORMATION

CALORIES 290

PROTEIN	5 g	CHOLESTEROL	61 mg
FAT	4 g	FIBER	4 g
SAT. FAT	0.5 g	SODIUM	350 mg

Today, most berries are never out of season. Don't be afraid to load up on berries—they're low in calories, high in fiber, and an excellent source of vitamin C.

BERRY SHORTCAKE

Makes 8 servings

6 low fat shortcake biscuits (I use reduced fat Bisquick mix)
2 cups assorted berries: strawberries, blueberries, raspberries, or blackberries
juice of 1 lime
1¹/2 cups fat free frozen strawberry yogurt or ice cream

Make the biscuits according to the shortcake recipe on the box. Slice the strawberries and mix with any additional berries.

Take ¹/2 cup of the berries and puree in a blender or food processor. Pass the berry puree through a fine strainer to remove any seeds.

Slice the biscuits in half. Place a scoop of the frozen yogurt or ice cream on the bottom halves of the biscuits. Top with the remaining berries. Place the top of the biscuits on the berries.

Serve with the berry puree.

NUTRITIONAL INFORMATION

CALORIES 320

PROTEIN	6 g	CHOLESTEROL	56 mg
FAT	9 g	FIBER	4 g
SAT. FAT	1.5	SODIUM	670 mg

I have always believed in getting kids involved in the kitchen. Assembling these kebobs is a great way to do so. Serve the kebobs as a side item with salads, sandwiches, or even for breakfast.

FRUIT KEBOBS

Makes 4 servings

8 10-inch skewers
16 strawberries
2 cups cubed melon—cantalope or honeydew
24 pineapple cubes
16 cubes of angel food cake
juice of 1 lime
4 sprigs of fresh mint, chopped

Arrange the fruit and angel food cake on the skewers. Squeeze the lime juice over the fruit, then sprinkle with mint.

NUTRITIONAL INFORMATION

CALORIES 130

PROTEIN	3 g	CHOLESTEROL	32 mg
FAT	1 g	FIBER	5 g
SAT. FAT	0 g	SODIUM	118 mg

Texture in food makes eating exciting. To start the day off right, add a little texture to your breakfast.

GRANOLA

Makes 12 servings
Temperature: 325°F oven

2 cups rice cereal
2 cups bran cereal
2 cups rolled oats (not quick-cooking or instant)
1 cup raisins or any chopped dried fruit
¹/₂ cup pecans, chopped
¹/₂ cup honey
2 tablespoons margarine, melted
2 teaspoons cinnamon
vegetable spray

Preheat oven. Spray vegetable spray on a nonstick roasting pan.

Combine the rice cereal, bran cereal, rolled oats, pecans, cinnamon, melted margarine, and honey.

Bake for 10 minutes, then remove from the pan. Mix in the raisins.

Stores well for 2 to 3 days in a tightly sealed container.

NUTRITIONAL INFORMATION

CALORIES 220			
PROTEIN	4 g	CHOLESTEROL	42 mg
FAT	6 g	FIBER	4 g
SAT. FAT	1 g	SODIUM	130 mg

You may want to save this parfait for dessert, but dig right in at breakfast to give yourself an energy boost that's loaded with calcium and vitamin C.

YOGURT PARFAIT

Makes 4 servings

2 cups plain low fat yogurt
1 cup sliced strawberries
1/2 cup blueberries
1/2 cup other sliced fruit such as grapes, kiwi, or orange segments
1 cup Granola (see page 187)

In a tall parfait or wine glass alternate layers of yogurt, granola, and fruit. Repeat until all the yogurt, granola, and fruit have been used up. Prepare the evening before and chill in the refrigerator.

NUTRITIONAL INFORMATION

CALORIES 200

PROTEIN	9 g	CHOLESTEROL	32 mg
FAT	4.5 g	FIBER	3 g
SAT. FAT	1.5 g	SODIUM	135 mg

Once sesame seeds are toasted, they have a great nutty taste. Serve the bananas with low fat ice cream or frozen yogurt. Or, for that occasional sweet-tooth indulgence, serve with this low fat caramel sauce.

SESAME BANANAS

Makes 4 servings

Temperature: grill or sauté high (bananas) medium low, then high (sauce)

4 bananas, cut into wedges
4 teaspoons sesame seeds, toasted
$^1/_4$ cup honey
2 tablespoons orange juice

CARAMEL SAUCE:
1 cup sugar
2 tablespoons margarine
$^1/_4$ cup fat free half-and-half
juice and zest of $^1/_2$ orange

In a small sauté pan add the orange juice and honey and boil. Toss in the banana wedges and cook for 1 minute. Then toss in the sesame seeds and coat well. Serve over frozen yogurt and topped with caramel sauce.

For sauce: in a heavy saucepan heat the sugar over the grill, stirring constantly, until it melts and becomes liquid. As soon as the sugar turns light brown, stir in the margarine and simmer for 15 to 20 seconds. Slowly add the half-and-half and simmer for 2 minutes over low heat. Stir in the orange juice and zest.

NUTRITIONAL INFORMATION

CALORIES 260			
PROTEIN	2 g	CHOLESTEROL	61 mg
FAT	3 g	FIBER	5 g
SAT. FAT	0 g	SODIUM	20 mg

The grilled pineapple will taste like heaven, so what else could go with it? Devil's food cake?—I don't think so!

ANGEL FOOD CAKE AND GRILLED PINEAPPLE

Makes 4 servings
Temperature: grill medium-low

4 slices angel food cake
1 fresh pineapple, peeled, cored, and cut into $^1/_2$-inch rings
$^1/_2$ cup orange juice
2 tablespoons honey
2 tablespoons sugar
$^1/_2$ cup frozen sliced unsweetened strawberries

In a medium bowl combine the orange juice, honey, sugar, and frozen strawberries. Lay out the pineapple rings in a pan. Pour the orange juice mixture over the pineapple and marinate for 30 minutes.

Pre heat the grill. Remove pineapple from orange juice mix. Boil the orange juice mix until it begins to thicken. Grill the pineapple until golden brown on both sides. Remove and lay the pineapple over sliced angel food cake. Pour the orange juice syrup over the pineapple and angel food cake.

NUTRITIONAL INFORMATION

CALORIES 190			
PROTEIN	2 g	CHOLESTEROL	47 mg
FAT	1 g	FIBER	2 g
SAT. FAT	0 g	SODIUM	210 mg

A balanced eating plan allows for a variety of foods. Even in moderation, this includes desserts. Lower the fat and you'll be surprised at what you can eat.

DESSERT PIZZA

Serves 6
Temperature: 350°F oven,
or according to package

2 packages low fat crescent rolls
1 cup low fat cream cheese
1/2 cup honey
assorted fruits, such as peeled sliced oranges, berries, grapes, bananas, etc.

Assemble the triangles of the crescent rolls on a round pizza pan. Arrange the triangles in a circle. Bake the crust and allow to cool.

Mix the honey and the cream cheese together. Refrigerate until ready to use.

Spread the cream cheese on top of the baked crescent crust. Arrange the fruit on top, then cut the dessert pizza into wedges.

NUTRITIONAL INFORMATION

CALORIES 320			
PROTEIN	8 g	CHOLESTEROL	41 mg
FAT	15 g	FIBER	3 g
SAT. FAT	3.5 g	SODIUM	210 mg

PART III:

THE 30-DAY
MENU PLAN

DAY 1

Motivation Tip

To reach the summit of the highest mountain requires taking the first step.

Fitness Tip

Keep a record or journal to chart your fitness progress.

Nutrition Tip

Besides adding flavor to foods, caramelized garlic may help prevent heart disease and cancer

BREAKFAST
1 cup orange juice
1 cup Special K
1/4 cup blueberries or raisins
1/4 cup plain low fat yogurt
1/2 banana
1 cup fat free milk
1 cup coffee

LUNCH
TUNA SALAD on whole wheat grain bread, lettuce, and tomato
10 baked potato chips
1 cup CARROT-APPLE JUICE
2 cups water

DINNER
salad with 2 Tbs CAESAR SALAD DRESSING
grilled ORANGE CHICKEN
medium baked potato with roasted peppers & basil
steamed broccoli with CARAMELIZED GARLIC and lemon
1 caffeine free diet cola
2 cups water

MID MORNING
1 nectarine
1 low fat Fig Newton
1 cup decaf tea
2 cups water

MID AFTERNOON
2 cups water
1 cup melon
1 cup decaf tea

MID EVENING
2 cups water
2 low fat OATMEAL COOKIES
1 cup low fat milk
1 cup decaf tea

DAY 2

Motivation Tip

Always aim for achievement and forget about success.

Fitness Tip

Stretching before and after workouts is the best way to prevent injury in any sport or physical activity.

Nutrition Tip

Substitute seasonal fruits for berries, nectarines, or melons.

BREAKFAST
1 cup grapefruit juice
1 cup oatmeal
2 Tbs raisins
1 Tbs sugar
1/2 banana
1 cup fat free milk
1 cup coffee

LUNCH
1 cup orange juice
1 bagel with low fat peanut butter & low sugar jelly
1 ounce pretzels
2 cups water

DINNER
greens with RANCH DRESSING
grilled PEPPERED SALMON STEAK
VEGETABLE ROAST
1 whole grain roll
1 caffeine free diet cola
2 cups water

MID MORNING
2 cups water
1 cup grapes
1 cup coffee

MID AFTERNOON
2 cups water
2 low fat Fig Newtons
1 cup melon
1 cup decaf tea

MID EVENING
2 cups water
1/2 whole wheat pita
1 slice low fat cheese
1 cup decaf tea

DAY 3

Motivation Tip

If you refuse to accept anything but the best, you very often get it.

Fitness Tip

Begin a workout with five minutes of light cardio activity prior to any light stretching.

Nutrition Tip

Fresh fruit, honey, and grains add texture and complement the taste of plain yogurt.

BREAKFAST
1 cup orange juice
YOGURT PARFAIT
2 slices wheat toast
1 Tbs low sugar jam
2 cups coffee

LUNCH
1 cup TORTILLA SOUP
lettuce, tomato, and 2
  ounces of low fat
  cheese on whole wheat
  grain roll
1/2 pickle
10 baked potato chips
1 caffeine free diet cola
1 cup water

DINNER
1 small salad
SESAME SEED DRESSING
BEEF FAJITAS
1 cup steamed brown
  rice
1 cup cooked carrots
1 caffeine free diet cola
2 cups water

MID MORNING
1 plum
2 cups water

MID AFTERNOON
2 cups water
1 cup melon
1 ounce fat free pretzels
1 cup decaf tea

MID EVENING
2 cups water
1 cup low fat milk
2 fat free cookies
1 cup decaf tea

DAY 4

Motivation Tip

What I eat today is very important, because a day of my life depends on it.

Fitness Tip

Advantages of strengthening your abs include better support of your back and decreased lower back pain.

Nutrition Tip

Nearly perfect food, beans provide forty-eight out of the fifty essential vitamins and minerals.

BREAKFAST
1 cup orange juice
2 whole grain waffles
2 Tbs raisins
2 Tbs low sugar syrup
6 ounces fat free yogurt
1 cup coffee

LUNCH
1 cup CLAM CHOWDER
1 cup orange wedges
bagel with 3 ounces of
   smoked turkey,
   lettuce, tomato, and
   mustard
2 cups water

DINNER
large salad with low fat
   vinaigrette
BLACK BEAN CHILI
1 cup rice
1 caffeine free diet cola
2 cups water

MID MORNING
1 cup fat free milk
1 banana
1 cup decaf tea
2 cups water

MID AFTERNOON
2 cups water
1 APPLE SMOOTHIE
1 cup decaf tea

MID EVENING
2 cups water
2 cups lite popcorn
1 cup decaf tea

DAY 5

Motivation Tip

The one who moves a mountain begins by carrying away small stones.

Fitness Tip

You are never too young or too old for physical activity.

Nutrition Tip

Bananas are a fruit athletes love; they contain approximately 100 calories each, mostly in the form of carbs that the body quickly converts to energy.

BREAKFAST

1 cup grapefruit juice
1/2 banana
1 English muffin with low sugar jelly
3 egg white OMELETTE with 1 slice low fat cheese
1 cup coffee

LUNCH

TUNA SALAD on whole wheat grain bread, lettuce, and tomato
1/2 pickle
10 baked potato chips
1 caffeine free diet cola
2 cups water
1 cup low fat milk

DINNER

1 large salad with BALSAMIC VINGER & BASIL DRESSING
1 PORK CHOP IN CACCIATORE SAUCE
POTATO SMASH
steamed broccoli with lemon
1 caffeine free diet cola
2 cups water

MID MORNING

6 ounces fat free yogurt
1/2 banana
1 cup coffee
2 cups water

MID AFTERNOON

2 cups water
1 plum
2 low fat Fig Newtons
1 cup decaf tea

MID EVENING

1/2 cup sorbet
1/4 cup berries
2 cups water
1 cup decaf tea

DAY 6

Motivation Tip	Fitness Tip	Nutrition Tip
Shoot for the moon. Even if you miss it, you will land among the stars.	Alternating muscle groups every other day may give you the best results with the least injury risk.	Strawberries are an excellent source of vitamin C, a good source of folate and potassium, low in calories, and high in fiber.

BREAKFAST
1 cup orange juice
1 cup bran flakes
1/4 cup strawberries
2 Tbs plain low fat
  yogurt
1/2 banana
1 cup fat free milk
2 cups coffee

LUNCH
1/2 cucumber, sliced
whole wheat grain roll
2 ounces regular cheese
1 cup grapes
BLACK BEAN & RICE SOUP
1 caffeine free diet cola
2 cups water

DINNER
salad with low fat
  ITALIAN DRESSING
SPINACH FETTUCINE with
  GRILLED CHICKEN and
  MUSHROOMS
steamed spinach and
  garlic
1 caffeine free diet cola
2 cups water

MID MORNING
1 English muffin with
  low sugar jelly
1 cup decaf tea
2 cups water

MID AFTERNOON
2 cups water
1 nectarine
1 cup decaf tea

MID EVENING
2 cups water
BERRY SMOOTHIE
1 cup decaf tea

DAY 7

Motivation Tip

Sacrifice is the foundation upon which progress and achievement are built.

Fitness Tip

Exercising five or six days a week should be done by rotating your training with different activities or sports.

Nutrition Tip

A serving of grapefruit contains less than 100 calories, and its high fiber content satisfies hunger.

BREAKFAST
1/2 grapefruit
1 bagel
1/4 cup blueberries
2 Tbs low fat cream
   cheese
1/2 banana
1 cup fat free milk
2 cups coffee

LUNCH
salad with YOGURT
   HONEY DRESSING
1 TURKEY QUESADILLA
10 baked tortilla chips
1 caffeine free diet cola
2 cups water
1 orange

DINNER
1 grilled turkey sausage
   with peppers, onions
   and mushrooms
1 cup pasta salad with low
   fat ITALIAN DRESSING
1 TOMATO ROAST PEPPER
   BRUSCHETTA roll with
   CARAMELIZED GARLIC
1 caffeine free diet cola
2 cups water

MID MORNING
1/2 cup orange juice
1 BANANA NUT MUFFIN
1 cup water

MID AFTERNOON
2 cups water
TOMATO JALAPEÑO LIME
   JUICE
1 cup decaf tea

MID EVENING
2 cups water
1 cup low fat milk
2 fat free cookies
1 cup decaf tea

DAY 8

BREAKFAST

1 cup orange juice
1 cup Cheerios
1/4 cup strawberries
2 Tbs plain yogurt
1/2 banana
1/2 cup fat free milk
2 cups coffee

LUNCH

ULTIMATE TURKEY
 BURGER on a whole
 wheat grain roll with
 lettuce and tomato
1 ounce of low fat cheese
1/2 pickle
10 baked potato chips
1 caffeine free diet cola
2 cups water

DINNER

MESCLUS SALAD WITH AHI
 TUNA
cauliflower with
 tomatoes
1 caffeine free diet cola
1 whole grain roll
2 cups water

MID MORNING

1 BANANA SMOOTHIE
1 cup decaf tea
2 cups water

MID AFTERNOON

2 cups water
1 plum
1 cup decaf tea

MID EVENING

2 cups water
1 pita pizza
1 cup decaf tea

DAY 9

Motivation Tip

The time is always right to do what is right.

Fitness Tip

Dress for your sport. If you look good, you will feel good.

Nutrition Tip

Whole wheat bread will contain mostly whole grain flour. Unless it states specifically on the label, "100% whole wheat," it may also contain refined white flour.

BREAKFAST
1 cup orange juice
EGGS ON THE RUN
6 ounces fat free yogurt
1 cup coffee

LUNCH
TUNA SALAD on whole
  wheat grain bread,
  lettuce, and tomato
carrot and cucumber
  sticks
10 baked potato chips
1 caffeine free diet cola
2 cups water

DINNER
1 salad with fat free
  RANCH DRESSING
SEARED BEEF ON A STICK
SWISS CHARD
SWEET POTATOES AND
  MARSHMALLOWS
1 caffeine free diet cola
2 cups water

MID MORNING
1 banana
1 cup decaf tea
2 cups water
1 cup low fat milk

MID AFTERNOON
2 cups water
1 APPLE SMOOTHIE

MID EVENING
2 cups water
CARROT NUT BREAD
1 cup decaf tea
1 cup low fat milk

DAY 10

Motivation Tip

One's finest achievements are the result of perseverance.

Fitness Tip

Travel is not an excuse not to exercise. Stay at hotels with fitness centers or find a gym so you can maintain your fitness schedule.

Nutrition Tip

Freeze grapes and bananas for a healthy, refreshing treat.

BREAKFAST

1 cup orange juice
3/4 cup low free
 GRANOLA
1 banana
1 cup fat free milk
1 cup coffee

LUNCH

3 ounces lean ham and
 low fat cheese on 1/2
 large whole wheat pita
 with lettuce & tomato
1 ounce pretzels
1 caffeine free diet cola
2 cups water

DINNER

BOK CHOY SALAD WITH
 SESAME SEED
 DDRESSING
MONKFISH STIR FRY
1 cup steamed rice
1 caffeine free diet cola
2 cups water

MID MORNING

2 fat free cinnamon
 graham crackers
1 cup decaf tea
2 cups water

MID AFTERNOON

2 cups water
1/2 cup grapes
1 cup decaf tea

MID EVENING

2 cups water
1 cup fat free frozen
 yogurt
1 cup decaf tea

DAY 11

BREAKFAST

1 cup orange juice
2 whole grain waffles
1/4 cup berries
2 Tbs low sugar syrup
6 ounces low fat yogurt
1 cup coffee

LUNCH

WHOLE WHEAT PITA PIZZA
1/2 cup raw broccoli
  with BLACK BEAN CHILI
  DIP
1 apple
1 caffeine free diet cola
2 cups water

DINNER

salad with low fat
  ITALIAN DRESSING
VEGETABLE SOUP
TURKEY KEBOBS
1 cup fettucine with 1
  Tbs olive oil &
  CARAMELIZED GARLIC
1 caffeine free diet cola
2 cups water

MID MORNING

1 banana
1 cup decaf tea
2 cups water

MID AFTERNOON

2 cups water
1 orange
1 cup decaf tea
1/2 cup cottage cheese

MID EVENING

2 cups water
1/2 cup SESAME BANANAS
  over 1/2 cup frozen
  yogurt
1 cup decaf tea

DAY 12

Motivation Tip

The difference between falling and failing is whether or not you get back up.

Fitness Tip

Work around injuries by performing exercises that do not irritate the affected area.

Nutrition Tip

Drink orange or grapefruit juice with the pulp as a substitute when a fresh orange is not available.

BREAKFAST

1 cup grapefruit juice
1 cup Special K
1/2 banana
1/4 cup blueberries
2 Tbs plain low fat
  yogurt
1 cup fat free milk
1 cup coffee

LUNCH

CREAMY POTATO TOMATO
  SALAD
whole wheat grain roll
  with low fat cheese,
  lettuce, & tomato
1 cup mixed fresh fruit
1 caffeine free diet cola
2 cups water

DINNER

SOUTHWEST TOMATO
  SALAD
PORK AND BEANS
1 large baked potato
1 caffeine free diet cola
2 cups water

MID MORNING

1 nectarine
1 cup decaf tea
2 cups water

MID AFTERNOON

2 cups water
10 mini rice cakes
1 cup grapes
1 cup decaf tea

MID EVENING

2 cups water
2 fat free cookies
1 cup low fat milk
1 cup decaf tea

DAY 13

Motivation Tip

Once you put your mind to something, you will find a way—unless you put your mind to finding an excuse.

Fitness Tip

Weight training increases bone weight and density.

Nutrition Tip

Always go food shopping after you have already eaten.

BREAKFAST
1 cup orange juice
1 cup shredded wheat
2 Tbs raisins
1/2 cup plain low fat yogurt
GRAPEFRUIT CRUNCH
1 cup coffee

LUNCH
1 cup TOMATO SOUP
low fat peanut butter and jelly on whole grain bread
1 caffeine free diet cola
2 cups water
1 cup low fat milk

DINNER
tomato & onion salad
GRILLED CHICKEN CUTLETS WITH ASPARAGUS
4 small boiled new potatoes
1 caffeine free diet cola
2 cups water

MID MORNING
2 cups water
1 cup coffee
fat free muffin
1/2 cup low fat cottage cheese

MID AFTERNOON
2 cups water
1 apple
1 cup decaf tea

MID EVENING
2 cups water
Berry Shortcake
1 cup decaf tea

DAY 14

BREAKFAST
- 1 cup orange juice
- 1 slice CARROT NUT BREAD
- 2 Tbs low fat cream cheese
- 6 ounces fat free yogurt
- 1 cup coffee

LUNCH
- VEGETABLE CHILI with 1/4 cup part skim mozzarella
- 10 baked tortilla chips
- 1 cup low fat milk
- 2 cups water

DINNER
- salad with RASPBERRY WALNUT DRESSING
- SWORDFISH ROAST
- 1/2 cup basil-flavored rice
- HOMINY, CORN, AND PEA SALAD
- 1 caffeine free diet cola
- 2 cups water

MID MORNING
- 2 cups water
- 1 banana
- 1 decaf tea

MID AFTERNOON
- 2 cups water
- 1 orange
- 1 cup decaf tea

MID EVENING
- 2 cups water
- BAKED CHOCOLATE APPLE
- 1 cup decaf tea

DAY 15

BREAKFAST
1 cup orange juice
FRITTATA
2 slices wheat bread
1 Tbs low sugar jam
1/2 cup blueberries
1 cup coffee

LUNCH
TUNA SALAD on whole
   wheat grain bread,
   lettuce, & tomato
10 baked potato chips
1/2 pickle spear
1 cup low fat milk
2 cups water

DINNER
salad with low fat
   ITALIAN DRESSING
STEAK ONION SALAD
portobello mushroom
1 whole grain roll with
   CARAMELIZED GARLIC
1 caffeine free diet cola
2 cups water

MID MORNING
2 cups water
6 ounces fat free yogurt
1 cup coffee

MID AFTERNOON
2 cups water
1 cup vegetables with
   RANCH DRESSING
1 cup decaf tea

MID EVENING
2 cups water
1 apple
1 cup decaf tea

DAY 16

Motivation Tip

Victory is not won in pounds, but in ounces.

Fitness Tip

An afternoon workout coincides with your body's natural energy peak.

Nutrition Tip

Vinegar is virtually devoid of calories, which makes it an ideal alternative to fatty dressings.

BREAKFAST
1 cup orange juice
1 cup Cheerios
2 Tbs raisins
1 cup fat free milk
1 cup coffee
1 banana

LUNCH
6 ounces grilled chicken with 2 Tbs CAESAR DRESSING & 2 cups salad
1 apple
1 caffeine free diet cola
2 cups water

DINNER
lettuce & tomato salad with BALSAMIC VINEGAR BASIL DRESSING
RED SNAPPER STEW
POTATO SMASH
WHOLE WHEAT FOCACCIA
1 caffeine free diet cola
2 cups water

MID MORNING
2 cups water
1 English muffin with low sugar jelly
1 cup decaf tea

MID AFTERNOON
2 cups water
2 fat free cookies
1 cup decaf tea
1 cup low fat milk

MID EVENING
2 cups water
1/2 cup sorbet
1/2 cup berries
1 cup decaf tea

DAY 17

Motivation Tip

You always pass failure on the way to success.

Fitness Tip

An afternoon work-out gives you an extra energy boost that lasts through the evening and will deter some of your appetite for dinner.

Nutrition Tip

Egg whites are an inexpensive substitute for egg substitutes.

BREAKFAST

1/2 grapefruit
1/4 cup egg substitute or egg whites, scrambled with low fat ham & cheese
1 whole wheat English muffin
1 cup coffee

LUNCH

SHRIMP ROLLUPS
10 baked low fat tortilla chips
1 caffeine free diet cola
2 cups water

DINNER

CUCUMBER ONION SALAD
PORK TENDERLOIN & ORZO
STUFFED EGGPLANT
1 caffeine free diet cola
2 cups water

MID MORNING

2 cups water
1 banana
1 cup decaf tea

MID AFTERNOON

2 cups water
6 ounces fat free yogurt
1 cup decaf tea

MID EVENING

2 cups water
ANGEL FOOD CAKE WITH BERRIES
1 cup decaf tea

DAY 18

BREAKFAST
1 cup orange juice
2 frozen pancakes
2 Tbs raisins
2 Tbs low sugar jelly
1/2 banana
1 cup fat free milk
1 cup coffee

LUNCH
TURKEY BURGER on
  whole wheat roll with
  lettuce and tomato
corn roast with 1/4 cupt
  black bean dip
10 baked potato chips
1/2 pickle
1 caffeine free diet cola
2 cups water

DINNER
PESTO TOMATOES and
  fresh mozzarella
VEGETABLE LASAGNA
whole wheat garlic
  bread
1 caffeine free diet cola
2 cups water

MID MORNING
2 cups water
1 cup melon
1 cup decaf tea

MID AFTERNOON
2 cups water
1 peach
1 cup decaf tea

MID EVENING
2 cups water
1/2 cup sorbet
1/2 cup grapes
1 cup decaf tea

DAY 19

Motivation Tip

A precious stone cannot be polished without friction.

Fitness Tip

Schedule time for exercise as you would for any other activity.

Nutrition Tip

Ounce for ounce, peppers are a better source of vitamin C than citrus fruits.

BREAKFAST

1/2 grapefruit
I cup oatmeal with cinnamom
1/4 cup berries
2 Tbs plain low fat yogurt
1/2 banana
1/2 cup fat free milk
I cup coffee

LUNCH

TUNA CHEF SALAD with fat free cheese, tomatoes, peppers, and cucumbers
I caffeine free diet cola
I cup grapes
2 cups water

DINNER

GREEK SALAD
CHICKEN ON A CAN
CORN ROAST
CHILI CORN BREAD
I caffeine free diet cola
2 cups water

MID MORNING

2 cups water
I cup orange juice
I slice carrot raisin bread
I cup decaf coffee

MID AFTERNOON

2 cups water
6 ounces fat free yogurt
I cup decaf tea

MID EVENING

2 cups water
1/2 cup frozen yogurt
I cup decaf tea

DAY 20

Motivation Tip

First you make your habits, then your habits make you.

Fitness Tip

Change the scenery to reduce boredom while exercising.

Nutrition Tip

Shellfish (shrimp) contain fewer calories, weight for weight, than other sources of animal protein.

BREAKFAST

1 cup orange juice
2 whole grain waffles
1/2 cup berries
2 Tbs low sugar syrup
1 cup coffee

LUNCH

VLT (VEGETABLE, LETTUCE, AND TOMATO)
1 ounce fat free pretzels
1 caffeine free diet cola
2 cups water

DINNER

SOUP IN A MINUTE
1 cup steamed rice
ASPARAGUS AND PEANUTS
PORTOBELLO MUSHROOM with SPINACH STUFFING
1 caffeine free diet cola
2 cups water

MID MORNING

2 cups water
1 BANANA SMOOTHIE
1 cup decaf tea

MID AFTERNOON

2 cups water
1 apple
1 cup decaf tea

MID EVENING

2 cups water
2 FRUIT CREPES with 1 cup berries
1 cup decaf tea
1 cup milk

DAY 21

Motivation Tip

We don't know who we are until we see what we can do.

Fitness Tip

Set goals in your daily fitness routine to improve your abilities.

Nutrition Tip

A small amount of carbs (like cereal with nonfat milk) about half an hour before bedtime will make you sleepy.

BREAKFAST

1 cup melon
1 cup Special K
2 Tbs raisins
1/2 banana
1 cup coffee
1 cup fat free milk

LUNCH

3 ounces of turkey on
  whole wheat bread
  with lettuce & tomato
10 baked potato chips
1/2 pickle
1 caffeine free diet cola
2 cups water

DINNER

SPINACH SALAD AND
  BEETS
fettucine with VODKA
  SAUCE
1 caffeine free diet cola
2 cups water

MID MORNING

2 cups water
1 cup orange juice
1 fat free granola bar
1 cup decaf tea
1 cup fat free milk

MID AFTERNOON

2 cups water
1 cup grapes
1 cup decaf tea

MID EVENING

2 cups water
3 cups lite popcorn
1 cup decaf tea

DAY 22

Motivation Tip

High achievement always takes place in the framework of high expectations.

Fitness Tip

Seek a mentor or trainer to refine techniques of a sport.

Nutrition Tip

Adding beans to meats as the centerpiece of the meal will provide the required protein—and be filling as well.

BREAKFAST
1 cup orange juice
1 cup shredded wheat
2 Tbs raisins
2 Tbs plain low fat yogurt
1/2 cup fat free milk
1 cup coffee

LUNCH
TURKEY BRUNSWICK STEW
1 whole grain roll
1 cup low fat milk
1 caffeine free diet cola
2 cups water

DINNER
CHOPPED GREEK SALAD
  with CUCUMBER ONION
  DRESSING
LEMON CHICKEN PASTA
1 caffeine free diet cola
2 cups water

MID MORNING
2 low fat graham crackers
1 cup decaf tea
2 cups water

MID AFTERNOON
2 cups water
1 apple
1 cup decaf tea

MID EVENING
2 cups water
1 FRUIT KEBOB
1 cup decaf tea

DAY 23

Motivation Tip

If you don't run your own life, somebody else will.

Fitness Tip

Join a gym or fitness program only after trying out the facility and talking to other members.

Nutrition Tip

One half-cup serving of cooked spinach provides more nutritional value than one-cup served raw, because it contains two cups of leaves.

BREAKFAST

1 cup grapefruit juice
3 egg white low fat cheese OMELETTE
2 slices wheat toast
low sugar jelly
1 cup coffee

LUNCH

GRILLED CHICKEN CAESAR salad wrapped in 10-inch tortilla
apple
1 caffeine free diet cola
2 cups water

DINNER

salad with low fat VINAIGRETTE DRESSING
STUFFED FLOUNDER WITH SPINACH
1/2 cup herb rice
1/2 cup steamed carrots
1 caffeine free diet cola
2 cups water

MID MORNING

1 cup water
1 cup low fat milk
1 banana
1 cup decaf tea

MID AFTERNOON

2 cups water
1/2 whole wheat pita with 1/4 cup HUMMUS
cucumber slices
1 cup decaf tea

MID EVENING

2 cups water
ANGEL FOOD CAKE AND GRILLED PINEAPPLE
1 cup decaf tea

DAY 24

BREAKFAST
1 cup orange juice
3/4 cup fat free
   GRANOLA
2 Tbs raisins
1/2 banana
1 cup fat free milk
1 cup coffee

LUNCH
1 cup VEGETABLE SOUP
VLT on whole wheat
   bread
1/2 pickle
1 cup melon
1 caffeine free diet cola
2 cups water

DINNER
ARUGULA WALNUT SALAD
TOMATO RICE WITH
   SMOKED SAUSAGE
SPINACH AND WALNUTS
1 caffeine free diet cola
2 cups water

MID MORNING
2 cups water
1 English muffin with
   low sugar jelly
1 cup decaf tea

MID AFTERNOON
2 cups water
2 fat free Fig Newtons
1 cup decaf tea
1 cup skim milk

MID EVENING
2 cups water
1/2 cup fat free frozen
   yogurt
1 cup decaf tea

DAY 25

Motivation Tip

What really matters
is what you do
with what you
have.

Fitness Tip

Avoid cocooning
by restricting the
amount of time
you watch
television.

Nutrition Tip

For optimum flavor,
ripe tomatoes
should be stored at
room temperature.
Once placed in the
refrigerator, the
flesh becomes
mealy.

BREAKFAST

1/2 grapefruit
1 cup bran flakes
1/4 cup berries
2 Tbs plain low fat
  yogurt
1/2 banana
1/2 cup fat free milk
1 cup coffee

LUNCH

TURKEY BURGER on
  whole wheat roll with
  lettuce and tomato
10 baked potato chips
1/2 pickle
1 caffeine free diet cola
2 cups water

DINNER

salad with fat free
  RANCH DRESSING
BLACK BEAN CHILI
1 cup steamed rice
10 baked tortilla chips
1 caffeine free diet cola
2 cups water

MID MORNING

2 cups water
1 BANANA NUT MUFFIN
1 cup decaf tea

MID AFTERNOON

2 cups water
1 orange
1 cup decaf tea
1/2 cup cottage cheese

MID EVENING

2 cups water
1 low fat fudge Popsicle
1 cup decaf tea

DAY 26

BREAKFAST

1 cup orange juice
1 bagel with low sugar jelly
1 banana
1 cup coffee

LUNCH

3 ounces of lean roast beef with SANDWICH SPREAD on whole wheat bread with lettuce and tomato
10 baked potato chips
1 apple
1 caffeine free diet cola
2 cups water

DINNER

MINESTRONE WITH SHRIMP VEGETABLE SOUP
AHI TUNA SALAD ON GREENS
POTATO AND TOMATO SALAD
1 caffeine free diet cola
2 cups water

MID MORNING

2 cups water
1 cup melon
1 cup decaf tea

MID AFTERNOON

2 cups water
1 BERRY SMOOTHIE
1 cup decaf tea

MID EVENING

2 cups water
1 cup hot chocolate, made with 8 ounces of low fat milk and 1 Tbs chocolate syrup

DAY 27

Motivation Tip	Fitness Tip	Nutrition Tip
View every obstacle as an opportunity.	"No pain, no gain," only works in professional sports; seek the advice of a physician for any discomfort.	Soups are highly nourishing. Whether made from scratch, served in your favorite restaurant, or store-bought, remember to avoid creamed varieties.

BREAKFAST
1 cup orange juice
1 cup Cheerios
2 Tbs raisins
2 Tbs plain low fat yogurt
1/2 banana
1/2 cup fat free milk
1 cup coffee

LUNCH
BLACK BEAN SOUP
3 egg white FRITTATA
TOMATO ROAST PEPPER BRUSCHETTA
1 caffeine free diet cola
2 cups water

DINNER
lettuce and tomato salad with ranch dressing
TURKEY BURGER with PAELLA RICE
1 caffeine free diet cola
2 cups water

MID MORNING
2 cups water
6 ounces fat free yogurt
1 cup decaf tea

MID AFTERNOON
2 cups water
1 cup frozen grapes
1 cup decaf tea

MID EVENING
2 cups water
1 low fat milk
2 fat free cookies
1 cup decaf tea

DAY 28

Motivation Tip

The greater your obstacles, the more glory in overcoming them.

Fitness Tip

Make a seasonal calender of fitness activities.

Nutrition Tip

Try pasta at breakfast with a small amount of Parmesan cheese for an energy-packed start to the day.

BREAKFAST

1/2 grapefruit
1 low fat muffin or 1/2 cup cooked pasta with 2 teaspoons of parmesan cheese
6 ounce fat free yogurt
1 banana
1 cup coffee

LUNCH

SHRIMP ROLLUP with lettuce and tomato
1 apple
1 caffeine free diet cola
1 cup low fat milk
2 cups water

DINNER

mixed green salad with fat free ITALIAN DRESSING
VEAL CACCIATORE
1 cup spinach fettucine
1 piece whole grain BRUSCHETTA
1 caffeine free diet cola
2 cups water

MID MORNING

1 cup water
1 cup orange juice
1 bagel with low fat cream cheese
1 cup coffee

MID AFTERNOON

2 cups water
1/2 cup fat free pretzels
1 cup decaf tea

MID EVENING

2 cups water
1/2 cup frozen yogurt
1 cup decaf tea

DAY 29

Motivation Tip

Prepare for your future; don't live in the past.

Fitness Tip

Park the car at the furthest point in the parking lot, and walk a few extra steps.

Nutrition Tip

Pecans are a flavorful, crunchy source of vitamin E.

BREAKFAST
1 cup orange juice
1 cup Special K
1/4 cup berries
2 Tbs plain low fat yogurt
1/2 banana
1/2 cup fat free milk
1 cup coffee

LUNCH
1 bagel with low fat peanut butter and low sugar jelly
1 orange
1 caffeine free diet cola
2 cups water

DINNER
ONION & POTATO SOUP
TURKEY AND PECAN SALAD
FOCACCIA
1 caffeine free diet cola
2 cups water

MID MORNING
2 cups water
1 fat free muffin
1 cup low fat free
1 cup decaf tea

MID AFTERNOON
2 cups water
1 fudge Popsicle
1 cup decaf tea

MID EVENING
2 cups water
1 cup mixed fresh fruit
1 ounce reduced fat cheese
1 cup decaf tea

DAY 30

≈≈≈≈≈≈≈≈≈≈≈≈≈≈≈≈≈≈≈≈≈≈≈≈≈

Motivation Tip

If you are going to be thinking, you might as well think big.

Fitness Tip

The twenty-minute-a-day workout rule is only a starting point; work up from there.

Nutrition Tip

When buying zucchini, look for ones that feel firm and heavy.

≈≈≈≈≈≈≈≈≈≈≈≈≈≈≈≈≈≈≈≈≈≈≈≈≈

BREAKFAST
1 cup grapefruit juice
2 whole grain waffles
1/2 cup berries
2 Tbs low sugar syrup
1/2 banana
1 cup coffee

LUNCH
1 cup VEGETABLE SOUP
SHRIMP CAESAR SALAD
1 cup melon
1 caffeine free diet cola
2 cups water

DINNER
mixed green salad with
   SESAME SEED DRESSING
CAVATELLI PASTA WITH
   TURKEY CHILI
zucchini with CILANTRO
   PESTO
1 caffeine free diet cola
2 cups water

≈≈≈≈≈≈≈≈≈≈≈≈≈≈≈≈≈≈≈≈≈≈≈≈≈

MID MORNING
2 cups water
6 ounces low fat yogurt
1/2 banana
1 cup coffee

MID AFTERNOON
2 cups water
1 orange
1 cup decaf tea

MID EVENING
2 cups water
2 CHOCOLATE OATMEAL
   COOKIES
1 cup decaf tea
1 cup low fat milk

≈≈≈≈≈≈≈≈≈≈≈≈≈≈≈≈≈≈≈≈≈≈≈≈≈

ABOUT THE AUTHOR

George Hirsch has always had a passion for adventure. His adventures began at the age of five on family outings. This would become more than a pastime; it would be the beginning of an adventurous way of life. From learning to cook from his Italian mother and grandmother to the chores his two sisters delegated, he developed self-discipline in his professional and leisure activities.

From his parents he learned the importance of sharing. This is evident as George shares his passions for cooking through the years as a professional chef and teacher. His father, a master gardener, taught him to stop and smell the roses. In George's martial arts training, he has learned from his Sensei the importance of a nonquitting spirit. The sensible nutrition that he practices supports his health and fitness activities.

As a chef, George has achieved tremendous acclaim. He is a graduate with high honors from the Culinary Institute of America, a certified executive chef and a culinary educator. The American Culinary Federation inducted him into the Academy of Chefs, the most prestigious honor society of chefs in the United States. He was the culinary director of the Culinary Arts Center at New York Institute of Technology, a fully accredited college-level culinary school. One of his most rewarding experiences is being cofounder and chairperson emeritus of the Chef and Child Foundation, a national program with over 20,000 American chefs dedicated to fighting hunger and emphasizing nutrition among the young. George serves on the Board of Directors of the Congressional Hunger Center in Washington, D.C. He is the recipient of many awards and honors, including the Humanitarian of the Year Award from the American Culinary Federation.

In spite of his outstanding accomplishments, George gives the average person the motivation to excel at any activity. In his hugely successful series on public television, he has shown his viewers how to celebrate health and fitness, cooking and nutrition, travel and recreation, and gardening. He is a major contributor to improving the quality of family life by involving all family members in the excitement of sharing the experience of better living. With his "guy next door" demeanor, George shows his viewers how to make living more active, healthy, and enjoyable.

Millions of viewers have seen George weekly on his national public television programs *Grilling with Chef George Hirsch, George Hirsch's Know Your Fire, George Hirsch for Better Living & Lifestyles,* and *George Hirsch Living It Up!* A global, interactive audience can also access George's programs via Centerseat.com on the Internet.

George is also the author of *Grilling with Chef George Hirsch, Gather 'Round the Grill, Adventures in Grilling,* and *George Hirsch's Know Your Fire.* George is also publisher of the weekly electronic newsletter *Chef George Hirsch's Recipes for Healthy, Active Living.*

Prior to his national television series, George owned and operated restaurants that showcased his talents. He was also the host of a weekly television segment on News12 Long Island. You may have also seen him on many local and national talk shows, such as *The Today Show, Good Morning America, Live with Regis and Kathie Lee, Crook and Chase,* and CNBC's *America's Talking.* As a natural down-to-earth teacher, George has shared his secrets with the Home Show, Our Home, CNN, TNN, Food Network, Disney Channel, Food Channel, and America's Health Network.

During interviews, you can hear the sizzle in his speech on national radio programs on NPR, WABC, CBS, USA Radio Network, and many regional and local stations. Periodicals including the *Washington Post, Dallas Morning News, Atlanta Journal Constitution, New York Times, Newsday, San*

Francisco Chronicle, Chicago Sun and *Tribune, Family Circle,* and *Good Housekeeping* have sought a taste of George's creative style.

However, it is with live public audiences that George begins to "ignite the fire." As a featured speaker, George was one of the first Artists in Residence at the Disney Institute. Known to entertain and educate his audience on television, George shares the amusing side of food, lifestyles, and travel. Travel with him to beautiful outdoor locations as he explores the latest in food, fitness, and just plain fun.

VISIT AND E-MAIL CHEF GEORGE AT:

chefghirsch.com

INDEX